T   ite

M000035304

Carol Wiggs
Dec '05

Fourth Down
&
Goal to Go

Fourth Down
&
Goal to Go

Pat Taylor

Edited by Edward L. Rankin, Jr.

Ivy House
Publishing Group
www.ivyhousebooks.com

PUBLISHED BY IVY HOUSE PUBLISHING GROUP
5122 Bur Oak Circle, Raleigh, NC 27612
United States of America
919-782-0281
www.ivyhousebooks.com

ISBN: 1-57197-432-6
Library of Congress Control Number: 2004107663

Printed in the United States of America

INTRODUCTION

Some ten years ago, Ed Rankin suggested that I write a book about some of my experiences in North Carolina politics and public life. Ed served as private secretary to Governor William B. Umstead and Governor Luther H. Hodges, and later as director of administration for Governor Dan K. Moore. He has a keen insight into North Carolina life and politics during the same period in which I served in the General Assembly and as Lieutenant Governor. With that background, if he thought my experiences and observations as a citizen, lawyer, politician and elected official during the past fifty years would be of interest, and a worthy subject for a book, I was persuaded that it might be worth the effort. After extensive discussion, several stops and starts, and with considerable help from Ed, who added some material based on his own experiences, here it is.

We have tried to give credit wherever it is due and known. Many of the speeches I made and that are included, in whole or in part, were written by others. Jerry Shinn, who later was editorial page editor and associate editor of *The Charlotte Observer*, wrote a number of speeches for me when I was Speaker of the House of Representatives and Lieutenant Governor. I would hasten to add that I believe everything I ever said or wrote, and I am grateful to those who helped me express my thoughts and beliefs better than I could have by myself. I don't think I am like the political candidate who concluded a campaign speech by saying, "And now, my friends, these are my sentiments and if you don't like them, I'll change them." Included are stories, humorous and serious, which have been favorites of mine for many years. Some readers, especially my friends, probably have heard them before. Eugene Pond, a veteran U.S. Coast Guard man who was one of my friends from down east, wrote me years ago: "Pat, that was a mighty good speech you gave down here and everybody loved it, but

I've heard some of those stories a hundred times, and wish you would go fishing and catch some more."

I have found that it is much easier to plan to write a book than to write a book. It reminds me of Fully Huntley from Wadesboro, a successful businessman who later was elected chairman of the board of county commissioners in Anson County. There was an annual Farm-City Day dinner sponsored by the county farm agency, and Fully, a special guest, was introduced by John Potter, the farm agent, with these words: "Mr. Huntley doesn't know anything about farming, but he and the board of commissioners have treated us well when we needed help." Fully replied, "I do know something about farming. Last year I bought a goat and found out it's a lot easier to buy a goat than it is to sell a goat."

I heard former Congressman Richardson Preyer tell a story that may be a good illustration of my vanity in undertaking this book. Judge Learned Hand was an eminent jurist who lived in New York and was noted, among other things, for turning down an appointment to the Supreme Court of the United States. In his later years, Judge Hand was asked what he thought Heaven would be like. The judge responded: "I really have never thought about it, but I think it would be something like this. You would get up, have breakfast and go fishing all morning. After lunch, you would play golf all afternoon. Then after dinner, there would be an assembly of 400 of the greatest intellects in the history of the world. Aristotle and Socrates would be on the stage and engaged in debate, and someone in the audience would interrupt them and say, 'Aw, you all sit down and let Judge Hand talk.'"

I have been prompted in this project to relate stories that ought to be preserved, of people who contributed to humanity and may not have been recognized or given credit for their efforts. I believe that it would be great if more people would leave a written record of their lives, their experiences and stories relating to their times. There is an old saying, "Every person has a story to tell and if they don't, it will die with them." In the post-Reconstruction period, a Richmond newspaper editor named William L. (Buck) Royall was asked to define his favorite reading. "Well, sir," he replied, "I have read the Bible with great care. I have put many of its beautiful passages to memory. I have read all the great classic works from Homer to Gibbon. I count the plays of Shakespeare among the finest works of man. I have not neglected contemporary writers, some of whom excel in wit and style. But I will say to you, sir, that for perfect pleasure and pure enjoyment, I know of no finer pastime than to go to bed with a half-pint of good whiskey and read my own editorials."

Yogi Berra, the baseball philosopher, was quoted as saying, "The future ain't what it used to be." I can't predict the future of North Carolina politics and public policy, but perhaps this book may help to explain, in ways small and large, how we got to where we are today at the dawn of the 21st century.

It is late in the fourth quarter for our generation. We have won a lot of games . . . and we have lost some . . . and others are being played today. If we don't score some big touchdowns, we won't win the Super Bowl and we won't win the right to be called the "greatest generation."

My Family and My County:

Some History and Geography

My Brothers, Frank and Pete

My parents came from eastern North Carolina. My father, Hoyt Patrick Taylor, was from Hertford County and my mother, Inez Wooten, was from Columbus County. They met after he graduated from Wake Forest Law School and came to Wadesboro to practice law, and she graduated from Woman's College (now UNC-Greensboro) and came to Wadesboro to teach school and find a husband, as was the custom in those days.

They had four children: Hoyt Patrick Taylor, Jr., Frank Wooten Taylor, Caroline Corbett Taylor and Pete Taylor. Pete was black. The rest of us were white.

When my brother Frank Wooten was four years old, it became apparent that his muscles were not developing in a normal manner. My parents took him to a number of physicians and hospitals, starting with Dr. Sedberry, who founded the Baby's Hospital in Wilmington, and ending with Johns Hopkins Hospital in Baltimore. The diagnosis was muscular dystrophy. Frank's muscles were not growing and developing with the rest of his body. The prognosis was death at a relatively early age. The illness itself does not kill, but it causes severe respiratory problems when the muscles of the chest will not allow the lungs to function properly. Frank was able to walk fairly well until the fourth grade, when he had to stop attending school. He spent the rest of his life in a wheelchair. He could not turn over in bed by himself, and therein lies the story of my brother Pete.

In the depths of the Great Depression, the Anson County Welfare Department consisted of one person, Miss Mary Robinson. She knew of a 12-year-old boy, Arthur Pittman, who had been abandoned by his parents. Arthur was black and needed a home and family. My parents agreed to take him into our home, where he helped care for brother Frank. Having no family, Arthur adopted the name of Pete Taylor and lived with us as a loving and beloved member of our family. We would all hang our stockings together at Christmas time and Santa Claus would visit us all. Pete was fully our brother.

Frank and Pete became close friends. Frank was smart, loved reading and music and never complained. He died on Christmas Day in 1958. He had developed a cold and the muscles in his lungs were not strong enough to cough up the congestion.

I remember one day riding on the bus to Charlotte with Pete, and the bus driver told Pete he could not sit with me, that he had to sit in the back of the bus. To this day I have regretted that I didn't go back and sit with Pete. I've never asked the Lord to forgive me because I didn't want Him to know about it.

Some years after Frank Wooten died, I received a letter from William Cross, who lived down east in Gatesville. At the end of the letter he wrote, "Many years ago while visiting my old friend, Bob Little, your mother and father had us to dinner. Whatever became of the little black boy you all were raising in a manner not understandable to people of the North?"

The answer to his question was that Pete went into the Army and became ill and died while serving his country.

A year or so after Frank's death, I was asked to be North Carolina chairman of the Muscular Dystrophy Association, and I was pleased to accept. My wife, Elizabeth Lockhart, and I were invited to visit the national association's offices in New York City. We stayed at a suite at the Essex House and dined in fine restaurants and saw the best plays.

It bothered me greatly that we were not shown or told about the ongoing research and treatment programs for muscular dystrophy. When I returned home, I resigned.

Forty years later, I don't believe there has been any breakthrough on this terrible disease, even though Jerry Lewis has made a great effort to finance research toward that goal. As I understand it, MD is genetic and is inherited from the maternal side of the family. To my knowledge, no one in my family, either before or since, has had the same problem.

Over There in World War I

My father served in the U.S. Army during World War I. He was sent to Fort Jackson, South Carolina, and assigned to the 371st Infantry Regiment, which contained all black soldiers and all white officers. This infantry unit was sent to France, where it distinguished itself in battle and was awarded a citation for gallantry in action. One black soldier from Anson County in the 371st was given the Distinguished Service Cross. My father was wounded in action and received a Silver Star and a Purple Heart.

To my surprise, and as Ed and I had almost finished writing this book, I read a book review entitled, "The Harlem Hellfighters: Afro-American Soldiers Who Fought for the Right to Fight for Their Country." According to the review, no American soldiers saw harder or more constant fighting or gave a better account of themselves, whether in the campaign at Chateau-Thierry, at the St. Michael salient or in the Argonne. What most people knew, but no one mentioned in those days, was a shameful truth. The 94th Colored Division served with the French Army because General Pershing refused to allow an all-black regiment to fight with the U.S. Army. One member of that division, Henry Jackson, single-handedly fought off a German platoon. Wounded 21 times, Jackson also managed to save another wounded soldier. He was the first

American awarded the Croix de Guerre, France's highest military honor. He was, however, denied America's Congressional Medal of Honor because he fought with French troops in the war, and the award is reserved for those in the U.S. military who fought for their country. I guess Jackson was fighting to help make the world safe for democracy. (*The Harlem Hellfighters: Afro-American Soldiers Who Fought for the Right to Fight for Their Country,* 2002.)

A history of the regiment in which my father served included this story: "On the morning the regiment left for France, a big Mississippian, who was standing near where the regiment marched by to entrain, swore and said, 'I'm done talking about niggers. These boys have been fine soldiers here, and if I ever get back from France, I'm big enough to lick any man who don't give 'em a square deal.'"

My father recalled that while the regiment was at Fort Jackson the soldiers were not taking advantage of the $10,000 life insurance policy offered by the government for about $1 per month. (I don't know what they were paid, but it couldn't have been much. At the beginning of World War II, soldiers were paid $21 per month, or as has often been said, "$21 per day once a month." Soldiers believed they were fighting to save this country and the world for democracy and not for the money. I wish our politicians today would fight for the same reason.)

When my father's regiment arrived in France and was moved to the front lines, close enough to hear the sounds and see the flash of German artillery, many of the soldiers suddenly started applying for the life insurance they had refused at Fort Jackson. The officers found that it was not because the soldiers wanted to make sure they would leave something to their loved ones if they died. It was because there was a rumor going around that the government wouldn't send a $10,000 man into front line combat because it had too much invested in him.

My father said that when the regiment returned to the United States, and as the troop ship approached New York harbor and the Statue of Liberty came in sight, one of the soldiers said, "Old lady, take a good look at me, because you ain't ever going to see me again."

Anson County, Then and Now

Anson County, where I have lived all my life, is bounded on the east by the Pee Dee River, on the south by South Carolina, on the west by Union County, although it originally reached much farther in that direction. It was named for a British admiral, Lord Anson, who was the first Englishman to circle the globe. In appreciation, the king gave him a grant of all the land west of the "Great Pee Dee" as far as there were inhabitants. The Daughters of the American Revolution said this meant all the way to the Pacific Ocean, because there were Indians everywhere.

It has occurred to me that the county might retain Senator John Edwards on a contingent fee basis to recover the land to which it is entitled. At the time this is being written, Senator Edwards is running for vice president of the United States. If he is not elected but could win Anson County's case, we could make him chairman of the board of county commissioners, which, with the county reaching all the way to the Pacific, would be almost as big a job as president of the United States. In addition, with his contingent fee, he would own one-third of the land.

Although Anson County never developed its property to the West

Coast, many of the counties of western North Carolina originally were part of Anson, including Mecklenburg, which is now the most populous in the state.

North Carolina stretches so far to the west that people in Cherokee are closer to five other state capitals than they are to their own. At an airport in Andrews, in the far western mountains of the state, a pilot told me that if I wanted him to take me to Manteo or to Canada, whichever he could get to first, he would take me to Canada.

Anson County has shrunk not only in area but also in population. It had a population of 28,000 in 1900, and in 2000 it had a population of 24,000. This lack of growth is attributable to a cotton economy. In the early part of the 20th century cotton was called King Cotton, and many people were needed to plant, chop and pick the crop. Most of those workers were black tenant farmers. When the boll weevil swept the cotton-growing South, it destroyed cotton as a profitable crop and many of the tenants moved north. In Anson County today, the population is approximately 50 percent white and 50 percent black.

When I was a boy, there were two banks in Wadesboro. My wife's father, Adam Lockhart, a fine man, worked for one of the banks. He was also a farmer. He would bank in the morning and farm in the afternoon, because the banks opened at nine A.M. and closed at two P.M. The employees spent the rest of the day trying to balance the books. Mr. Lockhart had lived through four depressions and fully expected a fifth one. There was a story about a young man who came to Mr. Lockhart at the bank and applied for a loan of $4,000 to build a house. Mr. Lockhart asked the young man how old he was and how much he had saved to pay down. The response was 40 years old and $400, to which Mr. Lockhart replied, "Son, I can't make you this loan, because at the rate you are going you will be 400 years old before you can pay the bank back."

That story might illustrate why Anson County hasn't changed much. It is worth noting that Wadesboro was the only county seat on US 74 between Asheville and Wilmington that didn't lose a bank during the Great Depression. When Terry Sanford was governor, he spoke to our Chamber of Commerce and said, "You might have been better off if you had lost a bank."

The out-migration continues. As more white and black students attend college, very few come back to their home county after graduation, because not much economic opportunity is available here. Some years ago a federally funded rural medical center was established in Anson County and a black director was appointed. Two black doctors and a black dentist were employed, and not a single one of these professional people would live in the county. One of the doctors told me that his wife said she would leave him if she had to live in Anson County. This was largely due to a lack of amenities and the lack of a compatible social life.

After agriculture, the textile industry was the principal employer. In recent years, however, the import of textile goods and the "offshore" production of many textile products have caused a dramatic drop in textile employment in Anson County.

Vincent Hughes owned a local textile company manufacturing thermal underwear. Wal-Mart, a major customer, told him if he didn't stop sewing his own garments and begin sending them "offshore" for sewing, his company would not be a competitive supplier, and he would lose Wal-Mart's business. This is a far cry from Sam Walton's original slogan, "Only in America." Mr. Hughes said it cost him approximately nine dollars an hour for the sewing in Anson County. I went with him to Haiti to help negotiate a contract there. The contract entered into was for fifty cents an hour. This contract was with the employer and I have no idea what he paid his employees. The plant in Haiti had approximately 400 employees working in a tin building with some circulating fans and no air conditioning. There were both men and women sewers, and it was hot as hell in that workplace. It might be described as "slave labor" approved and promoted by the U.S. government.

In the early 1980s, the Coors beer people, whose operations were located in Golden, Colorado, decided to build a brewery on the East Coast. They retained a firm in Rhode Island to recommend two suitable locations. One was on the Pee Dee River in Anson County, and the other was in the Shenandoah Valley of Virginia. There was a major effort by North Carolina and Anson County to win this industrial prize. Governor Jim Hunt joined in and Lauch Faircloth, later a Republican U.S. senator, but then a Democrat and secretary of commerce in the Hunt administration, was in charge of the campaign to persuade Coors to choose Anson County. The state highway department agreed to build the roads the brewery would need, and railroads agreed to build a rail line to the proposed site.

North Carolina's ace in the hole was U.S Senator Jesse Helms. The Coors family loved Jesse and his conservative politics. Jesse did all he could to help locate the plant in Anson County.

(A digression: President Ronald Reagan nominated one of the Coors brothers for a high government position. According to what I heard took place at the confirmation hearing, a questioning senator asked, "Mr. Coors, are you now or have you ever been a member of the John Birch Society?" Mr. Coors answered, "No, I am not now, nor have I ever been a member of the John Birch Society, but I would hasten to say that I believe in everything they advocate." The committee chairman thanked Mr. Coors for his appearance and said, "I am told that you make some mighty good beer in Colorado, and I come from a beer-drinking state, but I don't believe this committee is going to confirm you." And it didn't.)

All of the top officials of Coors came to Anson County for their first visit. We took them to see the proposed site. Lauch Faircloth was driving the lead car with Bill Coors, the company president, in the front seat. I was riding in the back seat. The Coors family was very well educated and refined. Mr. Coors asked Lauch, "What is this land going to cost us if we decide to buy it?" Lauch said, "I don't know, but you will get the short end in the trade." Mr. Coors did not reply.

During their visit, I asked one of the Coors executives if they would import mountain water from Colorado to make their beer. (It was widely advertised as being made from Rocky Mountain spring water.) He replied that Coors makes the best beer in America and not to worry about the water. If they had to, they could make beer just as good from ocean water. He may or may not have meant it.

Opposition to putting the Coors operation in Anson County came from an unexpected source. The textile plant owners and operators in the county opposed it on the theory that Coors would pay their employees more than the textile operators and thereby lure employees from the textile business. The textile people also encouraged the opposition of ministers and church people, especially Baptists, who believed that the proposed brewery would bring sin into Anson County. On the day that Lauch and I were taking Coors executives to see the property, we passed signs that read, "Coors Go Home" or "Keep Beer Out of Anson County." It was enough to make me cry.

At the time Coors was making a decision, I made a speech to the Anson County Chamber Of Commerce in which I quoted a well-respected member of Congress who said, "Washington has written off the textile industry." I asked what would happen to Anson County if the textile plants closed. I was not sure then that this prediction would come true, and our textile owners and operators surely didn't believe it. Twenty years later a half dozen of our textile mills have shut down.

The Coors management finally decided on the Shenandoah Valley site, and they bought land there. I think they may have built a distribution center there, but as of yet no manufacturing plant. After the Coors campaign was over, Lauch Faircloth told me that there was a story going around Raleigh to the effect that Anson County was seeking to employ an industrial development manager and they advertised the position. There were twelve applicants, and when the fourth applicant was interviewed they asked, "How long have you been in the industrial development business?" He answered, "Twelve years." "How many industries did you bring in during that period?" He replied, "None." The Anson committee said, "You're hired."

The Way We Were

When I was growing up in Wadesboro, during the Depression, we had a telephone, and when we picked up the receiver we would wait, sometimes longer than other times, and the operator would come on and say, "Number please." If we said, "The bank," she would ring the bank. She also would ring the bank if we said, "Number 1," because that was the number of the bank. If we said, "The drugstore" or "Number 2" she would ring the drugstore. Our number was 192 and my father's office was 89. If my mother was calling Mrs. Pruette, the operator might say, "She's playing bridge at Mrs. Hardison's." If the fire whistle blew, we would have to wait awhile and when the operator would answer we could ask, "Where's the fire?"

If we made a long-distance call, there was a minimum charge for a three-minute call, and my father would stand by with his pocket watch in hand and would announce the fleeting time: "Two minutes" at two minutes, and at two minutes and 59 seconds he cut off the conversation no matter who was talking.

Outside of town, most people were on party lines and anyone served by the line could listen to whoever was using the party line. It was not unusual for a caller to be interrupted in the middle of a conversation with someone's impatient question: "How much longer are you going to talk?" We could call the grocery store, give an order and have the groceries delivered at our house within thirty minutes. If you had a charge account, you didn't have to pay then, but if you didn't have an account, you did.

Once a day, the ice wagon, pulled by a mule, would come by our house. If we wanted ten pounds of ice, it was chipped off a large block, weighed, taken into our house and put in the icebox. Around six o'clock each morning, a local dairy farmer would put our milk on the front doorstep. The bottles were clear glass so we could see where the milk stopped and the cream rose to the top. My mother had a little utensil that she used to skim the cream off the top. I guess that was where the term "skim milk" came from.

In our yard was a pile of stove wood, which was bought from and delivered by a farmer in the county and used primarily in the stove.

In some respects, things were better than they are now. In summer, people would come to our house selling blackberries and blueberries and huckleberries. A box of blackberries was five cents. Huckleberries were a dime because they were smaller and harder to pick. Blackberry patches were often full of red bugs.

When I was a small child, everybody in Anson County was a Democrat except for the postmaster, who was appointed by a Republican president. We were taught that Hoover got us into the Great Depression and Roosevelt got us out. Many of those who had an automobile couldn't afford to buy gasoline and they would remove the rear wheels and tires and build a buggy, pulled by a mule. These strange vehicles were called "Hoover carts."

Saturday was the big day of the week. The farmers came to town, most by mule and wagon. They parked on what was called "the back lot," where there were horse troughs for the mules to get water. There was also a blacksmith who provided his services for the mules and horses. It was the only day of the week that country people came to town to buy provisions and tend to their business.

The county courthouse stayed open until six P.M. Lawyer offices were open all day on Saturday. The "picture show" was open from noon until 10 P.M. It would be full because Saturday was the only day the farm people could see a movie. I worked in the movie theater selling candy and ice cream by walking up and down the aisles. Whites sat downstairs, blacks upstairs. I knew several people who would come when the theater opened and stay until it closed. They were among my best customers. In addition to the Saturday movie, there was a serial film that would end with the hero hanging on the edge of a cliff and the villain stomping on his hands. This was designed to bring the customer back on the next Saturday to see how the hero would escape.

Saturday was not only a business day, it was a social day, and like a holiday for the country people.

Sundays were church days, and Sunday afternoons were for visiting, often on front porches that had swings and rocking chairs.

I knew people seventy years old or older that had never been out of Anson County. Many people had no radio, and if you had one you had plenty of visitors. *Amos and Andy, Lum and Abner, Gangbusters, Grady Cole, Little Orphan Annie* and *Lucky Strike Hit Parade* were favorites.

If I was driving down a highway following another car, and the driver of the car ahead was going to turn left, he would roll down his window and point his arm to the left. If he was going to stop, he would drop his arm toward the ground. If he was going to turn right, he would hold his arm up.

We always had a Christmas parade in Wadesboro. The last float would be a truck pulling a decorated, flatbed trailer with Santa Claus seated in a big chair, throwing candy to the children. The parade ended at the courthouse where Santa Claus would sit on the courthouse steps and greet the children. They would get in line, take turns sitting on Santa's lap and tell him what they wanted him to bring them for Christmas.

Our Santa Claus worked in a local beer parlor and must have been a good customer there, too, because he must have weighed close to 300 pounds. After having served for many years as Santa, he announced to the parade chairman that he was quitting. The parade chairman asked, "Clem, why are you quitting? You are the best Santa Claus we have ever had." Clem replied, "A little 12-year-old boy sat on my lap and I said, 'Ho, ho, ho, little boy, what do you want me to bring you for Christmas?' He said, 'I want a bicycle,' and I said, 'Ho, ho, ho, little boy, I'll bring you a bicycle.' Then he said, 'Look, you pot-bellied son of a bitch, you told me last year that you would bring me a bicycle and you didn't do it. I want to know if you are really going to bring me one this year!'"

A Lilesville Baseball Fan in New York

Lilesville is five miles east of Wadesboro. Although it is a very small town, it has produced a good number of prominent people, such as the Liles, Walls, Battles, Ingrams, Judge Samuel Spencer and Red Barber, the famous baseball announcer.

There were four good friends from Lilesville who loved baseball. They decided to go to New York City to see the Yankees play. After leaving Lilesville by train on Thursday night, they arrived in New York the next morning and checked into a hotel. Since they were not going to the games until Saturday and Sunday, they proceeded to party on Friday afternoon, and by suppertime one member of the party was in no condition to go out to eat, so they left him in his hotel room. When they returned about 11 P.M., their partner was missing. They looked up and down the halls and in the lobby and outside the hotel. He was not to be found.

About midnight he called and said, "Come and get me." "Where are you?" they asked. "In jail," he said. "What jail? This isn't Lilesville where there is only one jail. They have lots of jails up here, so we have to know which jail before we can come and get you." Their friend said, "I'll tell you what you do. Y'all go down to the lobby and one of you pee on the palm tree, and they'll take you to the jail I'm in."

The Father of Soil Conservation

All the food in the world comes from topsoil, which is a thin layer at an average depth of seven to eight inches over the face of the land. That layer, which is subject to erosion by wind and water and depletion by over-farming, and which we have paved over at a rapid rate, is all that stands between mankind and extinction.

The soil conservation program in the United States began in the 1930s when Franklin D. Roosevelt was president. Dr. Hugh Hammond Bennett, who was born in Anson County, was the first director of the program and became known as the Father of Soil Conservation in America. The first soil conservation project in America was in Anson County.

When Dr. Bennett retired, a big celebration was held in Wadesboro in his honor and people attended from all over the country. One that I particularly remember was the national president of the Kudzu Association. Kudzu had been brought into America—I think from Japan—to be used for soil conservation. If the people had known at that time what they know today, the kudzu man would have needed a bodyguard. (Kudzu spreads like wildfire.)

Each generation is a temporary custodian of our land and water, our natural resources, protecting them for generations to come.

Colonel Samuel Spencer

The most distinguished resident in the early history of Anson County was Samuel Spencer. He was born in Connecticut, graduated from Princeton and came to Anson County from South Carolina. When the Revolutionary War began, Spencer, a loyal subject of the crown, almost immediately joined the Whigs. He represented Anson County at the First Provincial Congress in New Bern in August 1774. He was one of the first three Superior Court judges elected under the Constitution of 1777.

Judge Spencer's death in 1794 was unique. In feeble health, he was sitting in a chair in his yard. Being bald, he wore a bright red cap. Turkeys have an antipathy for the color red. As he dozed and nodded his head, a turkey gobbler passing by was attracted by the bobbing red cap and attacked it furiously. The judge was struck around the head and face with the gobbler's heavy spurs, and fell from his chair. When members of the household reached him, Judge Spencer was dead.

Such was Samuel Spencer's national reputation that a Philadelphia newspaper noted the event with this verse:

> *In this degenerate age*
> *What host of knaves engage*

And do all they can to
Fetter braver men
Dreading that they should be free
Leagued with scoundrels pack
Even turkey cocks attack
The red cap of liberty.

Dr. Albert Coates said that Judge Spencer championed individual rights more effectively than any North Carolinian during the 1700s. (Dr. Albert Coates was a law professor at UNC-Chapel Hill and founded the Institute of Government. He was a greatly respected and prolific speaker and writer.)

Highways

Tom Coxe was a legislator from Anson County. A group of farmers called him, saying they wanted to talk to him that weekend about an important matter when he came home from Raleigh. He met with them that Saturday and they said, "Tom, it ain't gonna work to have mules and wagons and automobiles on the same road at the same time, and we want you to get a law passed that when the state builds a road for automobiles they will have to build another road beside it for mules and wagons and horses."

Mr. Coxe told me he thought it was foolish idea, but in retrospect, it would have been a great idea, because today we would have four-lane divided highways throughout North Carolina.

Anson County Morals

The movie *The Color Purple,* a highly successful movie by Stephen Spielberg, was filmed in Anson County. It was very exciting. At one place in the movie they needed a team of mules pulling a wagon. There was an old gentleman in Burnsville Township in Anson County who owned mules and a wagon and an assistant went to retain their services. The conversation went like this:

"Mr. Jones, I understand you have a fine set of mules and a wagon."

"I sho' does."

"I work for Mr. Spielberg and he would like to hire you and your mules and wagon to be in his movie."

"Ain't that a dirty movie?"

"No, sir. It is a modern movie."

"Look, I ain't gonna be in no dirty movie and my mules ain't gonna be in no dirty movie."

. . . and they weren't.

He's Chairman of the Board

I am told that in the early 1900s the most respected office holders in Anson County were its county commissioners. They were the highest elected officeholders that most people knew personally.

Anson County had three commissioners, two of which would be farmers and the third would come from Wadesboro, a good businessman or other prominent citizen. In this instance, Dr. Hart, a medical doctor and a good businessman, held the office and was named chairman.

The board decided to attend the National Convention of County Commissioners in Washington, D.C. They stayed at the Willard Hotel. The first day, one of the commissioners became separated from the other two. The lost commissioner stood in the front door of the Willard Hotel, asking people coming and going if they had seen Dr. Hart. Finally, someone said to the commissioner, "Who in hell is Doctor Hart?" To which he replied, "Everybody knows that Dr. Hart is chairman of the board."

Change

A few years ago, when life was less complicated and there weren't so many people and they lived further apart, there was more independence and less interdependence. The well in your yard was your water system. The outhouse was your sewer system. The garden was your grocery store. The shotgun in the corner was your police department. The bucket in your well was your fire department. There was no need for an interstate highway because a horse and buggy could travel as fast over a dirt road as it could on a four-lane paved road, and there was obviously no need for a highway patrolman or a gasoline service station.

Generation after generation of the same family lived in the same town or on the same farm, and grandparents helped their children take care of their grandchildren and their children took care of them. The small number of children who went to college would, after graduation, return home to help in the family business or help run the family farm.

All of that has changed. It is irrelevant whether the change is for the better. It is a fact of life.

An old man was celebrating his 100th birthday and a newspaper reporter said to him, "Mr. Jones, I guess you have seen a lot of change in your life." The old man replied, "I shore have and I've been against every bit of it."

It is human nature, if one is getting along pretty well, to resist change. But today almost all our needs are met by pooling our resources to provide services throughout the county, the city, the state and, in some cases, throughout the nation. So we either stand together or we fall together. We can only meet our common needs by working together.

ON THE CAMPAIGN TRAIL

Running for Office

Effective government depends on social and educational conditions that produce good leadership. A functioning democracy needs a fair share of the most capable people to participate actively in the process of government, and that especially means running for public office. It ought to be a major concern that more and more of our ablest and most talented people will not run for office. Some have no interest. Some are too busy. Others do not want to beg for the money that is more and more necessary to have any chance of being elected. I hate to hear anyone say, "I'm not going to have anything to do with politics. All politicians are crooked." If enough people take that attitude, it becomes a self-fulfilling prophecy. People who say that should be indicted and tried for treason.

But I understand that it is much more difficult to get involved today than it used to be, and that, too, ought to be a major concern. I ran for the legislature from Anson County six times, beginning in 1954 with the last race in 1964. Hal W. Little was a prominent citizen of Anson County. He had served several terms in the State House of Representatives and decided not to run again. He felt an obligation to recruit a successor. He asked me if I might be interested. If not for this, I might never have run for public office. About all I did was to have some cards printed up with my name on them and "I would appreciate your vote." There might have been a minimum amount spent for local newspaper and radio advertisements. I believe that local elections produce the best results and it gets progressively worse in elections at the county, state and national levels.

A prospective candidate for public office went to a friend who was given to very frank expressions of opinion. "Earl," he said, "I'm figuring on running for land commissioner against Uncle Bob Hawkins. Which one of us do you think has the best chance to get elected?"

Earl replied, "Well, it depends on which one of you gets out and sees the most people. If Uncle Bob sees the most people, you will win. If you see the most people, Uncle Bob will win."

Should Everyone Vote?

Every election year the news media and the politicians and political parties try to "get out the vote." We make it easier and easier to register and vote. The principle is that the more people vote, the more democratic the process will be. I believe the principle is flawed. Most people who are interested in voting will register and vote. People who have to be pressured to register will likely not vote, or not vote intelligently, or will be more easily influenced by candidates who might appeal to the voters' most selfish instincts.

A *Time* magazine essay in 1992, entitled "Hold it! Don't Get Out the Vote!" made this observation: "There are, of course, intelligent citizens of goodwill who also ignore politics. One of the glories of our society is that they can do so safely. The engineer, chemist or doctor hard put to keep up with the demands of his profession for study and knowledge, the artist, musician or scholar totally engrossed in her field—in a totalitarian society they would not be allowed to be apolitical. To advance in their professions they would have to join The Party and devote some time to propagandizing for it. In a democratic country a physicist can pass up on participation in politics in order to spend every possible moment pondering the structure of the atom, and may well serve society better by doing it."

This point of view can be the subject of a lively debate on the requirements of citizenship.

During the Vietnam War, we had another war—the rebellion of the young children. One of their complaints was that if you were drafted when you were 18, you should have the right to vote. So we lowered the right to vote to 18 and the records show that less than ten percent of those under 21 exercised their right to vote.

In the Clinton-Bush election in the 1990's, for the first time in history, less than fifty percent of eligible voters exercised their right to vote.

A Statewide Campaign

I can comment from firsthand knowledge on campaigning in North Carolina in a statewide race because I was a candidate for lieutenant governor in 1968 and for governor in 1972. I won the first campaign but lost the race for the Democratic nomination for governor in a vigorous campaign that ended with a second primary victory for Hargrove (Skipper) Bowles, Jr. James E. Holshouser, Jr. defeated Bowles in the fall election, becoming the first Republican to be elected governor of North Carolina in the twentieth century. Other North Carolina Republicans were elected to public office—to the United States Senate, to the Congress and to the North Carolina General Assembly. It was the beginning of the end of the "Solid South," and from that year on we would have real two-party competition at the state level in North Carolina.

You can have wonderful, unexpected experiences while campaigning. One day I was in my campaign office in the Sir Walter Hotel in Raleigh when my secretary told me that there was a Catholic priest to see me. When he came in, he introduced himself, reached in his pocket and handed me $300 in cash as a contribution to my campaign.

I was greatly touched and told him how much I appreciated the offer, but said I could not take it because I knew he couldn't afford it.

"My son," he replied, "a gift is not meaningful unless it's a sacrifice."

I was moved to tears by his words. He blessed me and left. I did not remember his name and it was reported as a contribution from a Catholic priest, which probably violated the law, but it was the finest contribution I ever received in my political career.

The Art of Winning & Losing Elections

How political campaigns are won and lost is a mystery. I have observed a group of men sitting in a smoke-filled room. One of the group is thinking of running for state office. A friend will urge him to run and will say, "Bill, you can win. I can carry western North Carolina for you." Another will say, "I can carry the Piedmont for you." Another will say, " I can carry eastern North Carolina." The truth of the matter is that most of them can't carry the vote of their own wife, much less anyone else, but it is amazing how an eager and ambitious "would-be candidate" believes everything they say.

Another fallacy relates to the editorial endorsements by newspapers. Every candidate loves to get one, but I am not sure it is helpful and it might even be harmful. Years ago, when I was Lieutenant Governor, I met Paul Simon, who was Lieutenant Governor of Illinois. He later ran for Governor and was defeated. He wrote me and said that every leading newspaper in the state had endorsed him and he still lost. We concluded that the public enjoys disagreeing with editorial writers and their endorsements could do as much harm as it does good. Paul later became a leading U.S. Senator.

Terry Sanford for President

In 1971 former Governor Terry Sanford decided that he wanted to be President of the United States. The Democratic Convention would be held in the summer of 1972. Terry asked his friends in the 1971 legislature to enact a law calling for a Presidential Preferential Primary for the spring of 1972. North Carolina had never held one before and I don't think we have since. Terry thought it would help his chances of being nominated if he could show the nation how much he was loved in his home state. The legislature obliged and it was held in early May 1972, the same time as the first primary for state offices. I was a candidate for Governor in the same election. Then something happened that Terry did not anticipate . . . George Wallace, Governor of Alabama and the political leader of the segregation forces, entered the North Carolina primary. The results were:

Shirley Chisolm (a prominent black leader)	61,723
U.S. Senator Henry R. Jackson	9,416
U.S. Senator Edmund S. Muskie	30,739
Terry Sanford	306,014
George Wallace	413,518

Wallace got more votes than all other candidates combined . . . and it ended Terry's presidential aspirations.

On the same day, I was a candidate for Governor and the results were:

Bowles	367,433
Hawkins	65,950
Hobby	58,990
Taylor	304,910

In the second primary the results were:

Bowles	336,000
Taylor	288,000

Consistently during their campaign, I had said that busing of school children and racial issues should not be a part of the campaign and that the Governor could not, and should not, do or say anything that would defy the law. My remarks prompted Terry to write me the following note during the campaign. The note has been in my safe ever since I received it. At this late date, I don't think he would mind my using it. *(See opposite page.)*

After the first primary, Wilbur Hobby, who was prominent in the AFL-CIO, endorsed me, as did Dr. Reginald Hawkins, who was a black leader, as did Hugh Morton, of Grandfather Mountain fame, who started late in the campaign for Governor, and withdrew before filing. He would have made a good governor. I still lost. It would seem that these endorsementst would help, but a study of many elections proves that candidates cannot transfer their support.

HON. PAT TAYLOR
WADESBORO, N.C.

DO NOT FORWARD
ABSOLUTELY
PERSONAL and CONFIDENTIAL

TERRY SANFORD

Pat—

7/15/72

Your comment about bussing
was a great, statesmanlike
statement. I applaud!

Terry

DUKE UNIVERSITY

Public Speaking

I was asked to make the principal speech at a Fourth of July celebration in Cabarrus County. It was an all-day affair at the Mt. Pleasant ballpark, with music, food, exhibits and other activities. The speaker's platform was a flatbed trailer where Arthur Smith and his country and western band played from 10 A.M. to noon. Ty Boyd was master of ceremonies, and there was a crowd of 1,500 in the stands.

When Arthur Smith and his band stopped playing at noon, Boyd told the audience, "This is all the music we are going to have. Now we are going to have the Fourth of July speech." The crowd erupted from the ballpark like a fire whistle had blown. Not more than 25 people stayed to hear my speech. So I opened my remarks by saying, "If I ever come here again I'm going to speak before the music is played—not afterwards!"

J. Elsie Webb, president of the Richmond County Motor Speedway, invited me to welcome fans to one of his big NASCAR races. Elsie was also a prominent politician, a great friend of Richmond County Sheriff Raymond Goodman, and a former member of the North Carolina State Highway Commission (now North Carolina Department of Transportation). He had played football at

Wake Forest, weighed about 300 pounds and loved his school. So he invited Dr. Ralph Scales, the president of Wake Forest, to give the invocation before the race started.

Now if there is any place people are not interested in a speech, it is at a NASCAR race. The drivers are waiting for the race to start and warming up their engines—RUD DUH RUD DUH—and the crowd is standing or milling around anxiously awaiting the start. Meanwhile, the area covered by the public address system is so large that when I said something it was about three seconds before it came out of all the speakers. So I was hearing my words boom out as I was saying something else. It got me mixed up.

I don't think that Dr. Scales had ever been to a NASCAR race before, and he was not too happy to be there. But he knew Elsie was a loyal Wake Forest alumnus who planned to give the university some money, so Dr. Scales did the best he could under the circumstances. The speedway had been plagued that week with rain. It had rained out the Thursday time trials, rained on Friday and looked like it was going to rain on the big Sunday race. The threat of rain had hurt attendance.

After my brief welcoming remarks, Elsie said, "Dr. Ralph Scales, the president of Wake Forest University, will now give the invocation."

Dr. Scales began: "Shall we pray. Dear Lord, we thank you for the sunshine, we thank you for the rain . . ."

Elsie turned to me and in a whisper said, "What in the world is he talking about—thanking the Lord for the rain that is about to kill my race? He don't know nothing about racing!"

Campaigning has convinced me that all politicians are divided into two categories, and this difference can be of some importance during a political campaign: There are those who drink liquor and there are those who do not drink liquor. People who drink liquor like to stay up all night and discuss the campaign. Those who don't drink like to have early morning campaign breakfasts. If you have to deal with both crowds, it is very hard on your health.

Highways and Politics

For many years highway contractors were the prime movers in financing gubernatorial campaigns in North Carolina. This was a logical development because highway construction involved the expenditure of more state funds for private business than any other sector of state government. In fact, the two most important services provided by state government are to educate our children and to build and maintain our state highways. Other services are important, of course, but education and highways certainly do overshadow everything else.

When I ran for governor, I had, by and large, the support of the highway construction industry. They asked me to make only one promise for their support: to oppose allowing state government taking over the building of state highways and to leave this process to competitive bids among highway contractors. I had no problem making that promise. I knew that the contractors were getting fat off state highway construction, but that it would be better, more efficient for private companies to do this work rather than depend on a state-employed workforce.

A lovable man named Clarence Stone, who came to the General

Assembly from Rockingham County, was a strong supporter of good highways and defended the state highway program consistently against the repeated calls by political candidates that "we must get politics out of building state highways." Stone recalled that political candidates and others had been saying this for years. "Why, it's like taking the football out of the football game," he exclaimed with a grin. "It is not practical or possible to do this."

He continued: "For example, I could go to China and get a chinaman who could not read, write or speak English, put him in an airplane and fly from Manteo to Murphy. Then I could bring him to Raleigh, lay a map of North Carolina on the table and that chinaman would put his finger on where every highway commissioner lived."

The State Department of Transportation and the state highway system are never without critics. This may be some proof of how important they are to the life of the state. Rep. Liston Ramsey (D-Madison), who was a former Speaker of the House, complained one time that his county was not getting its fair share of the state road-building program. He said the Department of Transportation had cut every sapling in Madison County, staked out every road in the county, and yet had not poured any concrete or asphalt paving in ten years.

Under the bidding system at that time, highway contract lettings were held in Raleigh at regular intervals during the year. Each contractor would come to the Sir Walter Hotel and get a room, and in each room there was a speaker connected to the public opening and announcement of the low bidders. It was obvious to most observers that road contractors would discuss the bids with each other, but this was not thought to be too bad because final bids and contracts had to be awarded by the State Highway Commission. And the State Highway Department provided the Commission with its own estimated cost of each project. As might be expected, the low bid often went to the contractor with forces, equipment, materials, et cetera, closest to the job site.

It was a tragic ending to this state system when the federal government moved in and some of our better-known contractors and citizens went to prison for price fixing. I always felt that most of the people involved, government and private, knew what was going on for a long time. I thought we had a good system of road building by competitive bids in North Carolina and got close to our money's worth in building state roads. However, the rules were changed and as a result many contractors did not have much defense in federal court.

Politics, Mountain Style

Stories about western North Carolina politics have a special flavor all their own. A congressman from a mountain district, who was married, had several children and was a devoted family man, unfortunately had a small weakness for pretty girls. One fall while Congress was in recess, the justice of the peace came to the congressman and said, "Mr. Congressman, I have a terrible problem on my hands. A mountaineer came down here with his daughter yesterday and took out a warrant against you for bastardy. He says you are the father of his daughter's baby. Now I can hold the warrant for a few days before turning it over to the sheriff to be served, but you better get some of your friends to go see that fellow and see if they can't talk him into dropping the charge."

The congressman expressed his appreciation to the JP for the advance notice and had some of his friends contact the irate father, but they were not able to work out anything with him. A week or ten days went by and the JP returned.

"Mr. Congressman, I've got to turn this warrant into the sheriff," he said, "because that old man is giving me down the country for not doing my duty."

The congressman asked for and was granted one more day of grace "so my wife won't hear about it from some other source." He went home early that afternoon, hugged his wife and said, "Darling, you are not going to believe what they got *us* charged with."

Voting the dead and long departed was not unknown in many mountain counties. The day after an election in Madison County, an old man was seen on a bench in downtown Marshall, crying like a baby. One of his friends came up and asked, "John, what's wrong?" The old man replied: "I just heard that my dear old daddy, who has been dead ten years, came back and voted yesterday . . . and he didn't even stop by the house and say hello."

Two men were in a graveyard one night getting names off tombstones so they could be voted in the coming election. They came to one for John Paul Jones Smith. One of the men said, "We can get several names off this marker—John Smith, John Paul, Paul Jones . . ." The second man said, "Now, wait a minute. If we are going to do anything crooked, I ain't going to have any part of this!"

The Charlotte Observer conducted a vigorous crusade against illegal electioneering in western North Carolina. The absentee ballot process required a voter to go before a justice of the peace or notary public and, in effect, have his signature notarized. There were many questions asked about whether this was being done legitimately. When I was making a political visit in Madison County, a fellow came up to me and said, "Pat, you don't know who I am, do you?" My reply to the Madison man, who was a JP or notary public, was, "Well, your face is familiar but I don't know that I can call your name." The man said, "I'm the man *The Charlotte Observer* got about absentee ballots." When I asked what he was accused of, this was his answer:

> *Oh, they said I voted some folks didn't even live in Madison County. Now, Pat, you know a man got the right to vote his children. I don't care where they live . . . if they have gone to New York*

or somewhere, he can speak for the family. But I was charged with not doing right by absentee ballots and they tried me.

And here is the rest of his story.

> *The day court began, the District Attorney had a stack of absentee ballots that I had notarized—and I knew he had 'em, I could see 'em there on the table. Well, I was on the stand and he said, "How many absentee ballots did you notarize during the last election?"*
>
> *"Oh, I couldn't tell you that. I didn't keep up with the number of them."*
>
> *"Well," he said, "was it 25?"*
>
> *"Oh, no, it was more than that."*
>
> *"Well, was it 50?"*
>
> *"Oh, no, more than that, probably."*
>
> *"Well, was it about 75?"*
>
> *"It was more than that, probably."*
>
> *The District Attorney finally said, "How about 269?"*
>
> *I told him I would settle for that.*

While I was campaigning around western North Carolina, an older mountain man took me around, and we spent all day seeing as many people as we could. I wear loafers and have worn them all my adult life. At the end of the day, my mountain friend gave me this advice: "Boy, the next time you come up here campaigning, you wear some shoes that got strings in them."

Mitchell County, tucked high in the mountains on the Tennessee border, has the reputation of being the most Republican county in North Carolina. Thad Eure, who was North Carolina Secretary of State for 51 years and is often described (by himself and others) as "the oldest rat in the Democratic barn," said many years ago that if Mitchell County ever voted Democratic he would ride a mule from Raleigh to Bakersville. He never took the ride.

Jay Robinson's father was chairman of the Democratic Party in Mitchell County for many years, and Jay recalled that there was to be a three-county election involving Mitchell, Yancey and Madison.

Three men from Madison came to Jay's home on a Sunday afternoon to see his father. Jay was just a boy then but he remembered the visit. (Robinson grew up to be a distinguished educator and UNC administrator.)

One man said, "Now, John, tell us how many votes you are going to lose Mitchell County by. Tell us right because it is important."

After some thought, Jay's father replied: "Boys, we will not lose Mitchell County by over a thousand votes."

The Madison visitors departed. But the week before the election, Mr. Robinson became worried about the outlook for the election and told Jay, "Boy, get in the car. We are going to Madison County."

They met with the three men in Madison and Mr. Robinson said, "Boys, things are not going so good in my county. We could lose Mitchell County by 1,200 votes."

With this news, one of the men leaped up and shouted, "Blankety-blank, John, why didn't you tell us that before? Now we have to change all those boxes!"

It is all in your point of view. To the partisan mountain Republicans or Democrats, there is nothing immoral about trying to steal an election. The other crowd is doing the same thing.

The late Dan K. Moore, former governor and state supreme court justice who was mountain born and bred, said one of his earliest memories was about local elections. His mother would tell him it was Election Day and he could not go to town because there would be "all kinds of cussing, fighting and maybe a shooting or two."

For many years, the state highway patrol served a unique role in law enforcement in many mountain counties. The sheriff was often poorly paid, understaffed and needed help from time to time, particularly during a hotly contested election. A veteran state patrol sergeant, who served many years in the mountains, said it was not unusual for him to receive instructions from the state board of elections in Raleigh on an election day. His orders would be to wait until the polls were closed and then go to the county seat and impound all the ballot boxes. The boxes would be hauled to the county jail and locked in a cell. Then the sergeant would sit in front of the cell door until representatives of the state board of elections arrived and settled the disputed returns.

At a political rally in the mountains I met an old lady, a loyal Democrat, who expressed her feelings about her party this way:

"I remember when Grover Cleveland ran for president. My daddy took me down to the telegraph office to get the election results. I've been a Democrat all my life. I feel about the Democratic Party like I do about my husband. Been married 51 years and I never thought about leaving him—but I started to shoot him six times."

America's Love/Hate Relationship
with the Government

Several years ago I was asked by Bill Ballard of WBTV to be a commentator on the night of the presidential election. Channel 3 carried a movie that night and every hour interrupted the movie for 10 minutes of comments on the election. This meant I had a 50-minute break. I happened to walk by the receptionist's desk where there was a telephone console that looked as if it could accommodate 100 telephone calls. The receptionist said to me, "Mr. Taylor, I don"t want to hurt your feelings, but every time you come on the whole switchboard lights up and everyone says, 'Get those damn politicians off and start the movie again.'" America seems to have a love-hate relationship with government. I suppose a part of it is the basic instinct we have to like freedom, and as regulatory government becomes more intense, "less government" is "best government."

There is a desire of every man to share in his own rule and some of the frustrations may be that we do not feel that we are sharing in our rule.

Winning and Losing

First, let me be clear: I like to win and I do not like to lose. I am a competitive person. It doesn't make any difference whether I am trying a lawsuit, playing cards, in a golf game, or watching my team play in the Sun Bowl or the Peach Bowl. I love competition and I like people who are good at what they are doing. I like to see success and be a part of it.

But in 1972, I lost an election for the first time, after winning many, and for the first time I had to think about losing, and why I lost, and it causes a person to become both analytical and philosophical—even now, after all these years.

There is a cost to winning. Champions in almost any field of endeavor must make certain sacrifices and exert certain efforts to achieve their success. Talent is a part of this, but as Thomas Edison once said, "Success is one percent inspiration and 99 percent perspiration." Ambition, persuasion, dedication and hard work are really at the heart of success.

The same thing that is true of an athlete, a scholar, a scientist or a businessman must also have some application in the political arena. No one would deny that hard work helps win an election. No one would deny that enthusiasm and dedication and a belief in what one is doing would be anything other than a real asset in a political campaign.

Campaigning on television or for television news requires a candidate to have or acquire acting skills to deal with this powerful visual medium. The better the skills the more effective the candidate's message will be delivered. With the help of communication professionals, the reach and impact of a candidate's campaign can be targeted to specific groups of voters and regions.

Most people are good citizens, living their lives on a day-to-day basis, enjoying the blessings of life and liberty in America, and rarely, if ever, realizing these blessings were either bought with a price or can be lost in a moment. A Pearl Harbor or a terrorist attack on New York and Washington should always bring this lesson home to all of us. The real tough job of the political party is to help Americans understand the critical issues of the day and to provide intelligent leaders to represent them in public office, from the courthouse to the White House.

A candidate today must employ professional marketing and advertising people who will help guide and direct the campaign. These are good people, but they are professionals who can also sell soap, breakfast cereal, SUVs or other consumer products. They measure their ability by their success in selling, and I have had experience in their field.

I can tell you that the political advertiser is no different from the commercial advertiser. Both are students of human nature. When I was a candidate, I never felt worse than when I was talking with these people. I felt cheap, dirty and miserable, and this is no reflection on these people because it is a business with them. But every time I thought about it, I thought that the slogan of their company must be, "To seem rather than to be."

A candidate must have access to polling of public opinion. I have used polls, too. I had a polling firm that was supposed to be the best in the country. I have no reason to believe it was not. I never did want a pollster, but everyone told me I would be foolish not to have one.

The reason I did not want a pollster was because of the falsity of the implication of having one. You are really saying, "I want to find out what people want to hear and that is what I am going to say." In other words, you will not be a leader. You will be a follower. In the final analysis, there may be some merit in the Machiavellian theory that anything justifies winning, or that before you can be a good governor, you have to be a governor, or to put it in its final form, you do or say anything to get elected.

And here is a cynical definition of the art of politics from Oscar Ameringer: "Politics is the gentle art of getting votes from the poor and campaign funds from the rich, by promising to protect each from the other."

Well, I simply do not believe that and never have. I will be content and happy with my party if it never wins another election so long as it advocates the things that I believe are right and will help ensure the continuation of the world in which I believe. The American idea was that all people have certain rights and that to take these rights away from the least was intolerable. It is not only a noble idea, but also a divine idea. It was born of an oppressed minority people who had a revolution in support of this cause. As time went by, this minority became a majority and a majority, consistent with human nature, has lost sight and lacks understanding of the very things out of which they attained their status.

America is great because America has been good, but America must remain good to maintain her greatness. Someone wrote a poem:

How a minority
Reaching majority
Seizing authority
Hates a minority.

Mark Twain said in *The Adventures of Huckleberry Finn*: "Hain't we got all the fools in town on our side? Ain't that a big enough majority in any town?"

Ibsen, in one of his plays, wrote, "A minority may be right, a majority is always wrong."

And this brings me to what I am trying to say. I am not sure that being with the majority is the object of politics. I am not sure that winning means success. What I probably believe is that the political party serves best that stands up for things in which it believes even though the pollster and advertising expert says that this is not the position to take.

I have been in politics because I believe that politics will determine not only the destiny of myself and my children and of this country, but also whether the world will survive and whether it will be a free world and a world that will recognize the dignity of all people and the brotherhood of man.

We like to win every election because we believe that by winning the election we can advocate these things in which we believe, but I believe it is better to lose with this type of belief than to compromise for the purpose of success.

I have no apologies for losing a political campaign because I never said one thing that I did not believe, and I never said anything that was designed to divide our people.

Political Parties

I believe in the Democratic Party because I believe that it has throughout our history come closer to advocating the cause of the minorities . . . the poor, the sick, the aged, the helpless, the black, the Jews, and you name anybody else that the majority tends to forsake, and this to me is the heart of politics and the heart of America and the heart of our system of government.

George Washington, our first president, was opposed to political parties. He thought they would lead to dissent and antagonism that would not be beneficial to a harmonious society. I believe he was right. In spite of George's feelings, political parties sprang up and by 1800 were going full tilt. In the election that year, Jefferson's Democratic-Republican Party and Adams' Federalist Party were fighting in the arena and this has continued until this day.

We have always had a two-party system, more or less. From time to time substantial third parties have arisen, but they came nowhere close to victory. Theodore Roosevelt's Bull Moose Party, Ross Perot, Ralph Nader, Pat Buchanan, Strom Thurmond, George Wallace and the Libertarians are all examples. These efforts arose out of dissatisfaction with both of the dominant parties. They could be called protest parties, and in close national elections their votes can be a deciding factor by taking away votes from one of the two major candidates. It might be well to give two ballots to third party voters, one of which could read, "If your candidate should lose, for which one of the major candidates would you vote?" And this vote would count.

What is the Republican Party and what is the Democratic Party and what is the difference? I have asked myself and many other people that question. I have never gotten a satisfactory answer from myself or others. I have concluded that most people are two-thirds one party, and one-third the other party, whatever that means. I think that is why so many people are now registered as Independent.

I was born a Democrat. My mother and my father were Democrats, and their mothers and fathers before them. They never suggested that I might have some choice in the matter. The same was true of my religion. All of my ancestors were Baptist and it was assumed that I would be a Baptist. I was never asked if I would like to join another church.

As a young child, I was told that President Hoover got us in the Big Depression and Franklin Delano Roosevelt got us out of it. That might have been right or wrong, or partially right and partially wrong, but when it came to politics, it is how things appear to be that counts. FDR was God and Hoover was the devil. North Carolinians loved the welfare programs of the 1930s. The Works Progress Administration (WPA), Civilian Conservation Corps (CCC) and federal spending were welcome gifts because the people were poor, unemployed and in need.

Here are a few economic indicators of how bad it was: the number of U.S. unemployed multiplied eightfold from 1.6 million in 1929 to 12.8 million in 1932, the business failure rate rose by half, prices of farm products fell by half, and industrial raw materials by 23 percent (Ferdinand Baudel Institute of World Economics, 1985). Under Democratic administrations, people saw their standard of living improving.

The Person or the Party?

I always took the position that I was voting for the party, not a person. It was like if I didn't like the preacher, I would not leave the church. In the 1980s, Jim Hunt and Jesse Helms were running for the U.S. Senate, and the state Democratic Party asked me to write a letter that they would mail throughout the state. It was based on a talk I had made during a political campaign and which expressed my views at the time and to which I still subscribe. This is what I wrote:

In recent years a political slogan has become very popular in America. It is "vote for the man, not the party." Usually the ones who give this kind of advice belong to the Republican Party . . . because they are a minority party, and if some people didn't vote for the man instead of the party, none of their candidates would ever be elected.

It sounds very reasonable, "vote for the man instead of the party." After all, it makes sense to vote for the best person for the Senate or for the state legislature, or for attorney general, or for president or for any other office. Nobody would suggest that you ought to vote for the least qualified person.

But I would like to suggest to you that it isn't as simple as that. And I would like to suggest that if we believe in the kind of political system we have had in this country for almost two hundred years, and if we believe in the party of our choice, then there is something to be said for the opposite slogan, "vote for the party instead of the man."

Obviously, if you have good reason to believe that your party's nominee for a particular office is dishonest, or immoral, or incompetent, you are not going to want to vote for him, and you shouldn't. But short of that extreme, in most cases the choice of the party in an election is more important than the choice of individual candidate.

If it were possible for us to know, as voters, with absolute certainty, the man who would best represent the things in which we believe, the choice would be easy. But if we are honest with ourselves, we have to admit that we are rarely able to make that kind of judgment with absolute certainty. No matter how much we read the newspapers or watch the news on television, or study the issues, it is usually impossible for us to know for sure which is the really best man or woman. One may be better looking than the other. One may dress better, or smile more sweetly.

One may make a better speech. You may agree or disagree with one or the other on specific issues. Very often political advertisements during a campaign have little or no relationship to the office that the candidate seeks or the qualifications of the candidate to meet these responsibilities. Very often the issues raised in a campaign by competing candidates are totally irrelevant.

In the long run, any candidate, if elected, will have to function within a framework of political reality. He will have to function in relation to his party and the other members of his party. He will have to function within the political system . . . the Congress or the state legislature . . . and within the limits of his official powers. And for this reason, the party that is in power is more important than the individual.

We have basically a two-party state and a two-party nation. We have a choice between the Democratic Party and the Republican Party. Those of us who have chosen the Democratic Party have done so because historically we believe it has offered us the best candidates, and because it has performed well when it has been given authority by the people, and because it stands with certain things that we believe in. The historical trust of the Democratic Party and what it stands for are more important than the individuals who are running for office.

What I am trying to say is that it may sound fine and logical and reasonable to say, "vote for the man instead of the party." But the truth is, you can't do that. You can't vote for the man and not the party. When you vote for the man, you are voting for his party, and for the people who control the party, and for a set of beliefs and principles.

And many times those things turn out to be a lot more important than the individual whose name is on the ballot. I tend to believe that in times of greatest crisis in this country, the people have turned to the Democratic Party for leadership. I also think the Democrats have answered with nobility and statesmanship.

The Democratic Party stands for certain principles: That the smallest individual is just as important under the law and under his government as the largest corporation; that one man's opportunity to earn a decent living for his family is just as important as a business' opportunity to earn a profit; that there is no difference between the constitutional rights for a poor man and those of a rich man; that monopolies and price-fixing are just as much a threat to the free enterprise system as socialistic theories are.

It seems to me that for a hundred years the Democratic Party has believed and practiced, "Help the individual citizen to live a better life and you will be helping business to prosper and the affluent to become more affluent."

I wouldn't encourage any voter to vote blindly for a straight party ticket. But it is just as blind to vote for an individual without regard to his party and what it stands for. Because when you vote for any candidate, you're voting for his party, too . . . and his party may have a lot more influence on what kind of government we have and what kind of state and nation we have than the individual candidate . . .

Cordially yours,
H. P. TAYLOR, Jr.

One of the most thoughtful responses to my letter came from Philip P. Godwin of Gatesville, a good friend, lifelong Democrat and former Speaker of the House of Representatives. His letter, dated 27 November 1984, was written after Jesse Helms defeated Jim Hunt in the U.S. Senatorial campaign. Here are excerpts:

I have been a Democrat all of my life, having been reared in a home where my father compared the Republican Party with outlaws; however, over the years the philosophy and beliefs of those in charge of the Democratic Party have changed so much that I am sure that if my father was living, he and I would be in agreement inasmuch as the party has left me and I have not left the party. I know this is an old ring and you have heard it many times, but it falls on deaf ears and no attempt is made within the party to hold the old-line Democrats or give them any desire to stay within the Party framework.

Since your battle with Skipper [Bowles], the Party was fractured and no real attempt has ever been made to perform the necessary surgery that would cure the ill, but those now in charge for the past eight years have forgotten the majority thinking of the Democratic Party. His philosophy has been that he could take the minorities and the left-wing thinkers and force out those who dare venture to the right, and that their support and beliefs were no longer needed within the framework of the Party. Where were they to go and what attempt has been made to bring them back into the fold? . . .

I think we both realize that in many instances the only time that you can truly express your feeling is in the polling places. Those who have been looked over, those who have been disregarded, those who feel that the Party no longer needs them have an opportunity to express themselves and that is what took place this month. The majority of the people expressed themselves to the extent that they were dissatisfied with the leadership and the political cronyism that has been going on for the past eight years. In order to cure the illness of the Democratic Party, the surgeon must start at the top or the root of the illness and not merely give aspirin to the masses.

I cannot accept the theory that I must vote for every Democratic nominee that is placed before me, and I feel that I am in the majority in my thinking.
Philip P. Godwin

Do we really need a two-party system? I don't think so. I would hasten to add, however, that I don't think our present system is a threat to the survival of our country, but I do believe it could be made far, far more efficient and effective and could guarantee that we will have a government "of the people, by the people and for the people."

In our country today, candidates don't win elections; they buy them.

Once elected, and as a general rule, anything the Republicans are for the Democrats are against, and vice versa. Our bipartisan system in the North Carolina legislature today is a disgrace to the name of good government. In a discussion with a long-time friend, Gordon Allen, who served in the legislature in the early 1970s and was drafted to return in the 1990s, I expressed that view and he replied, "I agree with you, but it's not me. It's all those others." The system may have turned him from a very fine legislator into a puppet of the system.

When I first went to the legislature in 1955, there were 49 Democratic senators and one Republican, B.C. Brock from Davie County, a fine older gentleman. There were no blacks and only one woman, Mrs. Grace Taylor Rodenbough from Stokes County, a real lady. The overwhelming majority of the members were conservative and the state budget was always balanced and at the end of every biennium there was a surplus. It was not spent, but allowed to grow so that it could be used from time to time for capital improvements, avoiding a bond issue.

All of our governors in the 20th century had been Democrats until Jim Holshouser, a Republican, was elected in 1972, and Jim Martin, a Republican, was elected in 1984. I know them both. In 1963, when I was Speaker of the House, I appointed Jim Holshouser vice chairman of a House committee, which was unheard of and much to the chagrin of Liston Ramsey, a "yellow dog" Democrat. I did it as a gesture of good will. Jim never thanked me. He may have suspected it to be some kind of trick to get the Republicans in some kind of trouble. Anyway, if Holshouser and Martin had been in the legislature as Democrats, they would have gotten along fine and would have voted in such a manner that you couldn't tell either of them from a Democrat.

Acting and Oratory

Public speaking is deeply imbedded in American life and continues to be tolerated. A number of years ago, I accepted an invitation to speak to a civic club in Charlotte. This was during a session of the legislature, and I simply did not find time to either choose a subject, much less a speech. I hurriedly picked up three old speeches and when introduced said, "I have three speeches with me. The best one takes twenty minutes, the second takes twelve minutes and the worst takes eight minutes. I am going to take a vote as to which one you choose." There was a unanimous vote for the eight-minute talk.

I have been a member of several civic clubs in Wadesboro, and each of them had a speaker every week. I must have heard the superintendent of schools and the county farm agent a dozen times each. It would have been far more enjoyable if they let the speaker tell jokes or discuss community problems.

Commencement exercises always require a speaker. The shortest on record may have been Clarence Darrow, the famous trial lawyer, who told the graduating class, "Get out of here and go have a good time." At the other extreme, a couple sent their son to Yale University. He graduated and his proud parents attended the commencement.

The speaker used the letters of Yale for his subject: Y stands for youth and he spent 15 minutes on the joys of youth; A for ambition, another 15 minutes; L for leadership, 15 minutes; and E for enthusiasm. The proud father whispered to his wife, "Thank God we didn't send him to the Massachusetts Institute of Technology."

In the political world, speeches—at least the usual long ones—are almost a thing of the past. Television marketing has taken over and the only speech heard from a candidate is a 45-second message prepared by his campaign organization based on the recommendations of his professional pollster, taking a strong stand on issues that appeal to a majority of the voters. There was a time when live debates between the candidates were considered decisive. Newspapers would frequently cover them closely. The famous Lincoln-Douglas debates are considered great moments in political history.

Public speakers must be prepared for the unexpected. During a campaign appearance in western North Carolina, I was speaking to a crowd in a school auditorium. Governor Bob Scott had also been invited, but sent his wife, Jessie Rae, who was seated on the platform with me. In the middle of my speech, I spied a gentleman wobbling down the aisle toward me. When he arrived at the podium, he stopped and said, "I don't give a damn about what you are talking about. I want to know what you're going to do for the veterans."

I said, "Go over and sit by Mrs. Scott and I will get to the veterans."

Jessie Rae, a political veteran, smiled and pointed to the chair beside her. Before ending my remarks, I praised the veterans but to no avail. My visitor was sound asleep with his head on the First Lady's shoulder.

Many years ago I was asked to speak in Salisbury at the annual Sportswriters and Sportscasters Dinner. Chris Shenkle, a very well known and popular sports announcer, was on the program and told about attending a banquet in New York City the week before. He was seated next to a Chinese man. Trying to make conversation, Shenkle said to him, "Likee soupee?" It turned out the Chinese man was a nuclear scientist and was the main speaker for the evening. He spoke for thirty minutes in flawless English. Returning to his seat, the scientist turned to Shenkle and asked, "Likee speechee?"

When I was an undergraduate at UNC-Chapel Hill, I heard a speech by Glen Taylor, who was a U.S. Senator from Idaho. He spoke in Gerard Hall and I learned a great deal about politics from him. Senator Taylor said he was a professional actor, performing with a traveling road company in Idaho. The company would put up a tent, give performances for a day or two and then move on.

One night it was raining so hard that the show was cancelled. Having nothing to do, Taylor was walking down the street and saw an advertisement for a political rally being held for the incumbent governor, who was running for reelection. He knew nothing about politics but decided to attend the rally. The governor was speaking to the audience and next to him on the stage was the state treasurer, who had a thick ledger book on the floor beside him.

The governor asked the audience, "Have you seen the new bridge built across Jones Creek just east of town?"

The audience nodded that they had.

"Do you know who's responsible for building that bridge?"

They all shook their heads.

"I did!" the governor said.

There was loud applause.

"Do you know how much money I saved the taxpayers on how it was built?"

All heads shook no.

"I saved you $132,416."

Then he turned to the state treasurer, who picked up the ledger book, thumbed through it, looked up and said with a big smile, "That's right, Governor." This was followed by prolonged applause.

Glen Taylor said to himself, "I'm going into politics. If an amateur actor can do as well as the governor, think what a professional actor can do." He ran for public office and later became a U.S. Senator in Idaho. Taylor came to national attention before overextending himself as a candidate on a third party ticket and has not been heard from since. However, Ronald Reagan and Shirley Temple, along with a few other actors, proved there was some validity to Senator Taylor's approach to politics.

A superior court judge, Will Pless from Marion, who later served on the Supreme Court of North Carolina, had a favorite story relating to actors. Friends who had heard it one hundred times would ask him to tell it again.

There was a traveling show in rural Oklahoma. On one Saturday afternoon the leading lady took sick. The director of the show sent to a barroom in town and talked a barmaid into substituting for the leading lady.

In the last scene, the villain enters the stage and shoots the leading lady, at which point the hero comes in and says to the villain, "What have you done?"

At that point, a drunk cowboy in the audience, crying like a baby, stood up and said, "What has he done? He's killed the only whore in Catoosa County. That's what he's done!"

In the mid-1960s I met Stan and Sis Kaplan in Charlotte and we became good friends. They owned a radio station, WAYS, known as Big WAYS, which at that time was dominating the radio market in that area. When I ran for lieutenant governor, and later for governor, Stan managed my advertising campaigns. He was skilled in advertising, extremely intelligent, unfailingly loyal and a valued friend and political ally. But he was also opinionated and outspoken, which meant he was sometimes controversial, which I feared was a potential problem on the campaign trail. He understood that, but he was enthusiastic and sometimes irrepressible. I once told him, "Stan, I'm trying to put you in the back seat, but every time I do, the next thing I know you are back in the front seat."

At that time, Jerry Shinn, an experienced journalist and writer, was working for Stan, and he took a leave of absence to write speeches for me. The speeches were great. My only problem was that I felt great delivering the speeches, but I felt dirty inside because I was taking credit for the work of someone else, even though I believed everything I said. In discussing this with Ed Rankin, he disagreed with me.

He served as a senior administrator for three North Carolina governors in the days when staffs and budgets were small, and speech writing came with the job. He calls it ghost writing. I call it plagiarism, but of a benign sort, and probably necessary.

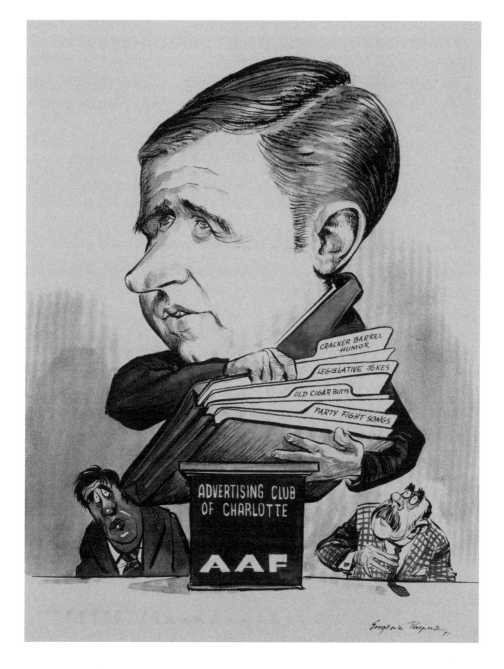

Appointments

Anyone who has ever been elected to a public office that has appointive powers knows the most unpleasant responsibility is making appointments. I have always said that those who deserve the least want the most.

President Abraham Lincoln had his problems with office-seekers and once told a whole group of them, who had waylaid him in his office, a story about an ancient king.

"This king," Lincoln said, "asked the minister who was head of the weather bureau if it was going to rain the next day, because he wanted to go hunting. The minister assured him that it would be a beautiful day. The next day the king and his party set out and as they rode along they met a farmer driving a jackass. The farmer warned the king that it was going to rain. The king laughed because he had the word of authority that it would be fair. The king rode on and as soon as he unsheathed his bow and arrow it began to rain, a torrential downpour that thoroughly soaked him.

He managed to get back to the palace, where he fired the weather minister and sent for the farmer.

"Tell me how you knew it was going to rain," he demanded.

"I did not know, your majesty," said the farmer. "It's not me. It's my jackass. He puts his ear forward when it's going to be raining."

The king sent the farmer away and commanded that the jackass be brought to the palace to replace the weather minister.

"It was here," said President Lincoln, "that the king made a great mistake."

"What was that?" asked one of the would-be appointees, falling into Lincoln's trap.

"Because ever since that time," said Lincoln, "every jackass wants an office."

No longer do those elected to public office have to worry about appointments. All they need to do now is to check who gave the most money to the campaign.

Ghost Writers

The Mayor of Chicago was reading a speech that had been written for him. There was a large audience. By accident the speechwriter had left out a page. When the Mayor finished page 4, the next page was page 6. The Mayor paused and then said, "Damn if I believe that myself."

An unnamed U.S. Senator had a hardworking staff assistant who wrote his speeches and the Senator would make a few handwritten changes such that it would make the original appear to be inadequate. On one occasion the Senator was reading and he got off to a magnificent start. Winston Churchill could not have done better. After he had completed the opening page he said, "and this, ladies and gentlemen, leads me to the five main points which I wish to leave you with tonight." He turned the page and it was blank except for a handwritten note signed by the assistant, "Now, you're on your own, big boy. I quit." When I was actively involved in politics I made many speeches that were written by someone else. I always felt guilty that it was plagiarism.

Country Lawyers

A Healthy Practice

I attribute my good health and happy life to living in a small town and country community. The house where I have lived most of my life is located some two blocks from my office, and my church is a block away. Within three blocks are the doctor, the hospital, the library and the post office. I can walk to work and to lunch. My law office is one hundred feet from the Anson County Courthouse. A few years ago I could have added, in similar proximity, the grocery store, the clothing store, the five and ten cent store, the drug store, the picture show and the automobile dealership. But since Wal-Mart and Food Lion arrived, downtown Wadesboro is almost deserted.

My friend, Charlie Knox, who is a city lawyer in Charlotte, will on occasion pick me up to go to Pinehurst to play golf. He will often say, "How do you live in this little biddy town? There's nothing to do, and if you do anything wrong, everybody in town will know about it before the sun goes down." I tell him we don't do anything wrong and we're happy and wouldn't think of trading it for Charlotte. The obituary pages prove that one lives a lot longer in Anson County than in Mecklenburg County.

I went to law school at UNC-Chapel Hill and in 1948 came to

Wadesboro to join the law firm of Taylor and Kitchin, which consisted of my father, Paul Kitchin and me. Wadesboro had a population of around 3,000 people, about the same as today. There were ten lawyers in Anson County, all located in Wadesboro with offices a half block from the courthouse. The other six towns in the county were blessed with no lawyers. All of the lawyers were white men. In law school, we had 73 students, all white men except for two white women, and I believe the women married lawyers who were in our class. I have a friend who is a senior partner in a large law firm. He said over a third of the firm were women. They have a tendency to be better lawyers than men.

It was not easy to practice law with my father. Our law office was on the second floor of a building on the square (the square means the center of town.) My father believed that a law office should not be on the ground floor because all the loafers would hang out there and waste a lot of our time. People started calling my father "H.P. Taylor, Sr.," to which he would always respond, "I'm not senior. That's not on my birth certificate. The boy can be junior if he wants to because that's on his birth certificate." He believed a lawyer should always wear not just a coat and tie, but also a hat. When we went out together, he would always ask, "Where's your hat?" knowing full well that I never wore a hat in my life. He believed there were only two holidays in a year—Christmas Day and Thanksgiving Day—and certainly not the day before or the day after. The office was open six days a week. At one P.M. on Saturday when I would tell my father that I wouldn't be in that afternoon, he would reply, "What's wrong? Are you sick or are you going out of town?" He knew that I wanted to play golf.

Most of the legal business consisted of writing deeds, real estate mortgages and chattel mortgages, domestic disputes and divorces, wills, and occasional criminal cases in county court. This was typical business for country lawyers. I must have written a thousand wills. Many a person has told me, "Pat, I need you to write me a will." But many of them died without ever making a will. It is easy to put off because it is not pleasant to think about dying. In most cases, a very simple will of two or three pages is fully adequate: "I will all of my property to my wife (or husband), if she is living at the time of death. If not living, I leave everything to my children. I appoint my wife (or husband) or children as executors of my estate."

Several years ago I came up with a great idea and tried it on a nice lady who had always been interested in her ancestors. I suggested that she write a codicil to her simple will and give advice to her children (not inconsistent with her will and to be sure to let me see any additions), tell them how much she loves them, and tell about her ancestors and any stories about them. I told her that after her death that her will would be recorded in the office of the clerk of superior court and would be there for eternity. I told her there was no extra charge for the length of the will and genealogists would love it. So did she, and she continues to make additions. Her will is three pages and her codicil is, at the time of this writing, eighteen pages long. Incidentally, when she comes in with her latest pages she will say, "Mr. Taylor, I've already paid you for my will, haven't I?"

In those days, malpractice suits were unheard of. Compulsory automobile insurance was not required until the 1960s, and there was no need to sue an insolvent defendant. Country doctors were about as poor as their patients.

It was not uncommon for a potential client to come to your office, sit down, talk for thirty minutes, thank you for your time, start to walk out and say, "Do I owe you anything?" If you had said "yes," he would have fainted. A lawyer had to write something before he was expected to charge a fee.

Willie Dunlap was a typical client. He was charged with drunk driving, not known then by the more sophisticated phrase, "driving while impaired." I had his case continued several times. This was not unusual. Finally, when it could not be delayed any longer and Willie had paid no fee, I said to him, "Willie, I hate to bring up this subject, but we got to talk about money today." He replied, "I'm glad you brought that up, Mr. Taylor, because I've just got to have ten dollars between now and Saturday."

I like to think that, in general, lawyers are respected, but I know that is not always the case. In part, this is due to the adversarial nature of the profession. I don't know that I ever represented a husband or wife in a domestic dispute without the other spouse holding hard feelings against me for life, particularly if the case was not settled amicably. There is a feeling that lawyers charge too much, and this is because the client doesn't think he or she should have needed a lawyer in the first place.

Physicians lose all their cases sooner or later, but when Mama dies all the family comes over and puts their arms around her doctor and tells him how much they appreciate all he did for Mama and how much she loved him. On the other hand, if Mama loses her lawsuit, the family comes over to her lawyer and says, "You son of a bitch, if you had done what you ought to have done, Mama would have won the case."

A number of years ago, I received an invitation to a meeting of Christian lawyers at Lake Junaluska. I showed it to a friend and he said, "There ain't gonna be many people at that meeting."

Paul Kitchin

Paul Kitchin married Dora Little from Wadesboro, and after a career in the FBI, he retired and the Kitchins moved to Wadesboro, where he became a country lawyer and went into law practice with my father. Later in life he was elected to Congress. He grew up in Scotland Neck, which is in Halifax County in eastern North Carolina. The county seat is the Town of Halifax. At one time it was temporarily the capital of North Carolina, and George Washington paid a visit there. My friend, Thorne Gregory, said that Halifax has been going downhill ever since.

Like my parents, Paul Kitchin had deep roots in eastern North Carolina, where the history of our state began, starting with the Lost Colony, the first English settlement, and Tryon Palace, where state government began under the auspices of the King of England. Plantations were common and the more affluent families became aristocrats. The area produced most of the political leaders of the state. There still prevails a feeling of superiority by eastern North Carolinians, particularly the landed gentry.

Eastern North Carolina has dominated politics in the state for many years, but with the population explosion in the Piedmont and the one-man, one-vote mandate of the U.S. Supreme Court in the 1960s, many of the far eastern counties were wiped out in the state legislature. The eastern legislators remained philosophical about it and one told me, "To hell with it. If they give Mecklenburg eleven representatives, five will vote one way and five will vote the other way and one will go to the bathroom so he won't have to vote." The easterners are still not doing too badly.

A number of years ago Elizabeth and I had friends, Mary Frances and Jimmy DeLoache from Dallas, Texas, who were visiting in North Carolina. Jimmy wanted to go to Northampton County where his forebears had lived. We drove down with them and on the way Mary Frances said, "You all talk about eastern North Carolina like it was another state. How am I going to know when I get there?" I told her that would be simple. "When you are introduced to someone and rather than saying, 'Pleased to meet you,' they say, 'Now, who was your mother?' or 'Who was your father?' you will know then that you have arrived in eastern North Carolina."

Paul Kitchin's grandfather was called Captain Buck Kitchin. He was the father of a North Carolina governor, of a president of Wake Forest College and of a congressman. He lived in Scotland Neck, which is in Halifax County. Captain Kitchin was a prominent man, but he had a serious shortcoming, in that he "cussed," not just a bit but a whole lot. The deacons of his Baptist church paid him an official visit and told him it was against the principles of the church to "cuss" and that as a leading citizen of the county he was setting a bad example, particularly for the young people. Captain Kitchin heard the warning but didn't quit, and he was formally "read out of the church."

This action was followed by several more meetings with the deacons, and finally Captain Kitchin agreed to stop "cussing," and he did, and peace was restored. A year later there was a district congregational meeting of Baptists in Scotland Neck, and Captain Kitchin was asked to make the main address. He was a fine orator and he accepted the invitation. When the Baptists assembled, he made a powerful speech on the history of Baptists in northeastern North Carolina, and at the close of his speech he got carried away and declared, "I may not be a Christian, but goddammit, I'm a Baptist!"

That story was told to me by Joe Branch, who married Paul Kitchin's sister, and who was as nice a man as God ever made. He also was a country lawyer, who later became a member of the North Carolina Supreme Court.

Chief Justice Parker

Another country lawyer who went to the state supreme court, and became chief justice, was Hunt Parker. He was learned, very dignified and some thought pompous. He would not read *The News and Observer* of Raleigh, but subscribed to a Richmond, Virginia newspaper. I was sitting next to Chief Justice Parker at the inaugural parade in Raleigh in 1969 when Bob Scott was sworn in as governor and I as lieutenant governor. It was an endless parade with many National Guard units participating. When the Halifax County National Guard unit marched by, the chief justice remarked, "Here are some real men. Their grandfathers fought at Appomattox and Gettysburg. Not a nigger in the crowd."

In this book, reference is made from time to time to the words "goddammit" and "nigger." They are words I never used, but they have been and are used, in the case of the latter not so much now as in the past. I do not mean to offend anyone, but it would be hypocritical to try to hide or ignore the fact that such language is, unfortunately, part of our history.

Contingent Fees

When I started practicing, lawyers did not advertise. It was considered to be unprofessional and degrading to the profession. Then the Supreme Court ruled that advertising could not be outlawed, and today lawyers advertise in newspapers, billboards, telephone directories, radio, television, et cetera.

Contingent fees are commonplace in personal injury cases, and the standard fee is one-third of the recovery if the lawyer files suit, and one-fourth if the case is settled without going to court. If there is a serious question of liability, the contingent fee may be justifiable but otherwise, the injured party is entitled to the amount of his or her actual damages and to take a third of this does not seem to be justice. If my $3,000 car is a total loss and a jury returns a verdict for that amount, it doesn't seem right for me to only get $2,000. It would seem fairer for the client to keep the $3,000 and in addition, let the jury decide what a reasonable fee for the lawyer would be, based on the time he spends on a case, and no more. I have been involved in cases where other lawyers are associated and a contingent fee was charged, but in fifty years I have never taken a case on a contingent fee basis.

There was a fine lawyer in Wadesboro, Banks Thomas, who years ago represented a client who was hit by a car while walking along US 74. I don't think he had it on a contingent fee basis, but he settled the case and called his client in to his office. Mr. Thomas had written the checks, had them on his desk and showed them to his client. He explained, "This check is for the doctor and hospital, this one is for you and this one is for me. What do you think about it?" The old man replied, "Sir, you would think it was you who got hit by the car rather than me."

North Carolina has a longstanding law that requires various professionals to pay an annual fee for the privilege of pursuing their occupation. A lawyer must pay $50 a year, for which he is sent a license that is required to be posted in his office. In fifty years, I have never seen one of these licenses posted in a lawyer's office. I have always posted mine in a closet. But the law reads that it must be posted "conspicuously." The law also says that each day a lawyer fails to comply constitutes a separate offense, subject to a penalty of $25 per day. In a year that would amount to $9,125 per lawyer.

If the state revenue department would retain a lawyer on a contingent fee basis to enforce this law, the lawyer could hire people to visit daily the offices of all professionals to which the law applies, to check for licenses conspicuously displayed. It would be a bonanza for the lawyer and for the state.

Courtroom Follies

Mr. Winslow, a very distinguished lawyer from Rocky Mount, told of this experience in the very old days. He represented a client who had a case pending before a justice of the peace in Battleboro, a small town located several miles from Rocky Mount. It was a civil case before the local justice of the peace, who ran a country store.

On a cold winter day, Mr. Winslow drove his horse and buggy to Battleboro. When he entered the store he said, "Good morning, Judge."

"Good morning to you, Mr. Winslow."

"It's a mighty wet and cold day."

"It sure is," replied the justice of the peace.

"I don't know anything better than to have a drink to warm you up, and I have a pint of whisky in my briefcase," the lawyer said. "Would you like a drink?"

To which the judge replied, "No, thank you, Mr. Winslow. I have already drunk with the plaintiff."

In a small rural community in the mountains of western North Carolina, an old woman had shot and killed her husband. While she was charged with murder, everyone knew that her husband had been about as sorry as they come. They knew that he mistreated his wife, provided little support and stayed drunk most of the time. Public support was 100 percent in her favor. The district attorney agreed that she could plead guilty to aggravated assault, and the judge had agreed upon a suspended sentence.

The case called for no evidence on the part of the defendant, but her young lawyer was anxious to call witnesses on her behalf. He had a woman who had been a long-time neighbor called to the stand and asked her these questions:

Lawyer: Do you know Mrs. Jones?

Witness: I shore do. Known her 35 years.

Lawyer: Do you know her general character and reputation?

Witness: I shore do. She's one of the finest women ever lived around here. Everybody loves her.

Lawyer: Do you know her reputation for telling the truth?

Witness: I shore do. She said she was going to kill that SOB and she did.

Thereby making a case for premeditated murder in the first degree.

I represented Tom Taylor, who had two charges of murder against him, one for killing his wife and one for killing his wife's sister. He shot both of them in front of his house in the Wade Mill Village. We entered a plea of something less than the electric chair. Judge John D. McConnell, a fine gentleman from Moore County, was presiding. I was pleading for leniency. In his sentence, the judge said, "Mr. Taylor, I can understand part of what you are saying. Every married man has some good reason to shoot his wife, but I can find no grounds for leniency for shooting his sister-in-law."

Judge Hamilton Hobgood, a well-respected lawyer and judge from Louisburg in Franklin County, was walking down the street in his hometown on a Saturday morning. This was in the days when farmers came to town on Saturdays, and he ran into an old friend of his, a farmer, wearing overalls. Judge Hobgood said, "Good morning, Robert."

Robert replied, "Good morning, Judge. I would like you to meet my cousin, Dr. Jones."

The Judge said, "Glad to meet you, Dr. Jones. Where do you practice medicine?"

Robert hastened to say, "Oh, Judge, he ain't that kind of doctor. He's a 'rithmetic doctor."

Dr. Jones was a professor of mathematics at the University of Richmond.

Marshall Cooper, president of Harriet Henderson Mills, had more than enough experience with lawyers before and after the extended and bitter strike at his company. "The next time I need a lawyer," he said, "I'm going to get a one-armed lawyer. Every time I went to see a lawyer, he takes his left hand and points in this direction, and takes his right hand and points in that direction, and says, 'You can do this or you can do that.' Hell, I knew that before I came to see him."

The North Carolina Bar Association held its annual convention one year on an ocean liner cruising from Morehead City to Bermuda. It took about a week. Bennett Perry, a very dignified older lawyer from Henderson and the uncle of Bob Kitrell, upon his return was asked how he enjoyed the convention.

His reply: "How would you like to be locked up in a nightclub for seven days and seven nights and couldn't get out?"

An old man in his wagon, pulled by his mule and with his dog beside him, was riding down a country road about dark when an automobile hit him from behind. The old man brought suit for the personal injuries he sustained and the case came to trial. The attorney for the defendant asked this question: "Is it true that you told the highway patrolman who investigated the case that you were not hurt?"

"Yes, sir."

"And now you are up here in court claiming that you are entitled to $10,000 in damages?"

"Yes, sir."

"Can you explain that, and if so, how?"

"Yes, sir. That patrolman came out to the wreck and my mule was lying in the ditch with a broken leg and the officer took out his pistol and shot my mule. He then went over and looked at my little dog that had a broken back and he shot my dog. Then he came over to me and said, 'John, are you hurt?' and I said, 'No, sir. I ain't hurt a bit.'"

The Law of Outer Space

The practice of law has changed dramatically since I started. Country lawyers, like country doctors, are things of the past. Specialization has taken over, with the help of computers, which now do everything. My beautiful law library can be put on five discs. I still like to read law out of a book.

I feel a little bit like I felt after hearing a speech by an expert at a bar meeting:

"Today I will speak on the law of outer space. Before I can speak on it I must define it. My best definition is, take all of space that there is and subtract inner space and what you have left is outer space."

How We Started, Where We've Been, and Where We're Going

Carolina got its name from King Charles the First. The name Carolina is from the word "Caroleus," the Latin word for Charles. It seems to be human nature to want something named for you.

Originally, Carolina included all of the land that now comprises both North and South Carolina, but in 1710 the king divided it.

Our state started on the East Coast and as the years passed people moved toward the West. The ports at Norfolk and at Wilmington supplied the immigrants.

The first four counties were Pasquotank, Perquimans, Chowan and Currituck, in the extreme northeastern part of the state. Our first capital was in New Bern, at the headwaters of the Neuse River. The British built a state capitol building there known as Tryon Palace.

Our major development, however, came from Wilmington in New Hanover County. When that county became fully inhabited, a new county was created to its west and is known as Bladen County and it acquired the name of the "Mother County." If Bladen is the "Mother County," New Hanover is the "Father County." The custom of forming new counties was to survey the eastern, northern and southern boundaries, but on the west it would say, "as far west as the state extends." As time has passed North Carolina has grown to 100 counties. The last was created by taking the western part of Cumberland County and creating Hoke County.

What Is a County and Why Do We Need Them to Begin With?

One answer is that a certain number of people will not obey the law. We call them criminals and if you have criminals you need a sheriff and deputy sheriffs . . . and you need a jail to put them in and a courthouse to try them in. In addition, we found that you needed to keep records relating to deeds and mortgages and births and deaths and marriages, so each county needed a register of deeds. We also needed someone to keep a record of civil and criminal cases and wills and estates, and so the clerk of court needed an office in the courthouse. All of this costs money so the tax collector needed an office . . . and finally you needed a place to try cases and so there was a courtroom.

Where did you place the courthouse? Obviously, in the center of the county. Transportation was a major factor in the early days when the only way to travel was by horses, mules, ox and wagons. We decided early on that every citizen should be able to leave home in the morning, travel to the courthouse and return home by nightfall. The general consensus was that 15 miles should be the maximum distance.

We had a state, we had counties and the next to come were towns. Until recently there were country stores throughout a county. They were similar to what we call convenience stores today. At night, the men in the community would gather there to talk, play checkers or "set back." Every candidate for public office would visit those stores. When they would walk in, all the talking and playing would cease and they would just stare at you . . . even though they knew you and why you were there. They enjoyed making it tough on a candidate. I found a great deal of wisdom in those people. They had time to read and think.

Towns came into being. That's when you could get supplies and services not available at the country store. Doctors, dentists, lawyers, hospitals, hardware stores, clothing stores, drug stores, etc. Most of the towns were on the railroad tracks where the trains brought supplies and traveling salesmen. There are seven towns in Anson County and every one was on the railroad track.

Chub Seawell

Chub Seawell was a lawyer of a sort, a Republican from Moore County, a fine gentleman and noted as a humorous speaker and writer. As a lawyer, he was a strong advocate of his clients but he had little patience for or knowledge of procedural matters.

On one occasion, he appealed a case to the Supreme Court of North Carolina. When the case came up for argument, Chief Justice Hunt Parker had looked the case over and procedurally it was a perfect mess. He sternly asked Chub, "How did this case ever get up here?" Chub answered, "I guess it came on the Southern Railway, because I mailed it from Carthage."

Chub enjoyed writing letters, often about political topics, to newspaper editors and to other publications. Here are some quotes from an article he wrote for *The State* magazine:

> About as far back as I can remember political activity was about 1916. The political cry back then was vote for Wilson and Peace or Hughes and War. Nobody wanted war so we all voted for Wilson, and it wasn't six months before war broke out. After the war, everybody said back to normalcy with Harding so we voted for Harding, and ain't nothing normal since then. Then along came

Calvin Coolidge and he wrinkled up his mouth and his nose and says the country as a whole is prosperous, and he just laid the ground floor for Herbert Hoover. Then along came Hoover and he cried Prohibition and Prosperity, and he hadn't been in office twelve months before we abolished both of them.

Then along came Cousin Franklin Roosevelt and he stood in the middle of Beacon Street in Boston and cried in a loud voice and says, "I hett waar, I hett waar," and we ain't had nothing but waar ever since.

Then along came Sir Harry the Trumanite and he said he was going out and give them hell, and he was right, we have had right much of it every since. Then along came Cousin Dwight David Sir Galahad Eisenhower, and he says what this country needs is a firm foreign policy and a balanced budget and when he got in instead of balancing the budget, we raised the ceiling and he appointed a man named John Frosty Dulles as Secretary of State, and he flew around the world and somewhere along the way he lost the foreign policy and we haven't been able to find it yet.

Then along came Cousin John Kennedy and he says think not what your country can do for you but think what you can do for your country, and they shot him. After that came Cousin Lendum Billions Nimrod Fountain Pen Benlah Land Father Divine Lyndon Johnson, and he stood on the Capitol steps with his arm around the Right Reverend Martin Luther King and in a mournful tone says, "Come unto me all that loot and are heavy laden and I will give you rest."

After the Great Society got fully established along comes Cousin Nimrod Nebuchadnezzar Nixon and he went to China and came back speaking Chinese. The first things he said when he got back were these beautiful words in Chinese: "hob le hoc choc cholly la dungi dungi babwi hin dut," which being interpreted means, "I done froze everything."

In the meanwhile, Cousin Billy Jeremiah Graham was preaching in the White House and trying to teach everybody to sing "I will meet you in the morning just inside the Eastern Gate," but the unbelieving, intellectual, atheistic White House aides got mixed up and got to singing to each other a new song entitled "I will meet you late tonight just inside the Watergate."

So as an honest historian, I am bound to say that when I think about politics I am reminded of the judge who sentenced a man to die and asked if he had anything to say. The man says, "Yes, Your Honor. No doubt a lot of people around here respect Your Honor, many folks look up to Your Honor and some folks may love Your Honor, but you done and ruint yourself with me."

As far as I am concerned, politics has done and ruint itself with me. (The State Magazine.)

ANNEXATION

Keeping Cities Healthy

Every town and city in North Carolina was incorporated by the general assembly; each act set its boundaries by law. But unlike the state and county lines, town governments soon found a need to expand or change their boundaries. When I first went to the legislature in 1955, many cities and towns were growing by leaps and bounds and the original boundaries set by the legislative act were antiquated.

In my opinion, and I think in the opinion of most people who have given any thought to the matter, if property which adjoins a town has the same needs for which the town was originally founded, then it should be made a part of the town, provided the town can offer the same services to its new inhabitants that it offers to its old inhabitants. To put it more concisely, areas that are urban should be municipal. Our present North Carolina annexation law is based upon this premise.

I found, in numerous incidents, a town would ask the legislature to extend it city limits, and then busloads of people who opposed the extension would come to Raleigh. They would fill the legislative halls, carrying posters of protest. Little did they know how the legislature

A strong annexation law is one of the main reasons why North Carolina's cities are among the fastest growing, have the most vibrant economies, and have the most fiscally sound city governments in the country, according to urban expert David Rusk of Washington.

Rusk, the former mayor of Albuquerque, N.M. regularly gives speeches to chambers of commerce and municipal officials in Chicago, Detroit, Philadelphia, Minneapolis and elsewhere. And wherever he goes he tells them "to learn how to organize to do business like North Carolina."

Since the 1950's, the American dream was to own a little house in the suburbs with a yard to mow, swings for the kids and a barbecue on which to grill the steaks. As the middle class migrated to the suburbs, businesses followed. Left behind were the poor folks . . . often Black and Hispanic.

Downtowns in Detroit, Newark, Camden, N.J. and elsewhere are abandoned hulks. There are no sadder sights this side of Calcutta.

But in North Carolina, thanks to The Nations' Best Urban Policy, the cities have grown and absorbed the new subdivisions, shopping centers and suburban office parks into the city limits.

"North Carolina has had the same patterns of growth as the rest of the country . . . very spread out, low-density growth," Rusk said. "But North Carolina law, more than any other state, encourages your cities to expand with that growth so that Raleigh, Greensboro, Charlotte and the like, take into their boundaries much of the new development that occurs."

In most cases, residents about to be annexed pitch a fit. Who wants to pay city taxes, especially when you can take advantage of urban amenities for free? But in North Carolina, cities can annex adjoining areas even if the people living there don't like it.

What would Raleigh look like without North Carolina's strong annexation law? Would the city be frozen at the Beltline? Would it be surrounded by new incorporated towns called Millbrook, Crabtree or Brentwood?

In his new book, Cities Without Suburbs, *Rusk provided a tale of two cities, Raleigh and Richmond, which are headed in different directions. One city was helped by a strong annexation, and one wasn't.*

The number of people living in the Raleigh and Richmond metro areas grew by the same amount from 1950-90. But because Raleigh was allowed to expand its city limits, Raleigh gained 142,272 people while Richmond lost 27,254 people.

In 1950, Richmond was three times Raleigh's size in square miles. Now Raleigh is significantly large. (Raleigh grew from 11 to 88 square miles from 1950-90.)

Raleigh is gaining manufacturing jobs, while Richmond's manufacturing base is shrinking. The income of Raleigh residents is growing faster than those who live in Richmond. The income gap between Richmond and its suburbs is growing. There is no such gap in Raleigh.

Richmond is showing signs of a city in decline. The Raleigh-Durham area recently made the cover of Fortune Magazine *as the nation's "Best City for Business."*

Sometime far-sighted laws come about in funny ways. The general assembly passed The Nation's Best Urban Policy in 1959, in part because it wanted the public off its back.

Before 1959, the legislature had to approve every annexation, which meant hundreds of spitting-mad citizens descending on Raleigh every year. Faced with a problem, the legislature did what it always does ... it formed a study commission, which with the help of the Institute of Government in Chapel Hill, drafted The Nation's Best Urban Policy.

The key figure in passing the annexation law was state Rep. Pat Taylor of Wadesboro, a 35-year-old lawyer who would rise to become House Speaker and Lieutenant Governor.

Was it controversial?

"Oh, my Lord," Taylor, now 70, said last week. "People said this bill was undemocratic. In truth, it couldn't be fairer."

The annexation law, Taylor said, will be one of his lasting legacies.

I don't know for sure, but I bet Taylor is the only lawyer in Wadesboro (population 3,801) who can claim to be the father of The Nation's Best Urban Policy.

I was particularly pleased that Wadesboro in 2002 increased its population from 3,801 to 6,000, using this law and with a minimum of controversy.

Our State Capital

Raleigh became the state capital because it was centrally located both geographically and in terms of population. When the new city, located in Wake County near Wake Crossroad, was laid out in 1792, the city contained 400 acres, including the streets, and 126 lots of one acre each. The area was nestled in a fine oak forest at the time and became known over the years as the City of Oaks.

Five public squares were reserved . . . Union, Caswell, Burke, Nash and Moore. The town commissioners also named the streets and began to sell off the lots, the proceeds going into a fund to build a statehouse on Union Square. A modest wooden capitol building was erected and the legislature met for the first time on December 20, 1794. Richard Dobbs Speight was the first governor to occupy the new capitol.

The first capitol building was completely destroyed by fire in 1831. The general assembly authorized construction of a new structure to be built primarily of locally quarried stone. Supervising architect, David Paton of Edinburgh, Scotland, recruited skilled masons from the North to shape the blocks of granite hauled to the site by a mule-drawn railroad, the first in North Carolina. The first appropriation by the general assembly was for $50,000, but the building finally cost $531,000, three times the annual revenues of the state.

Governor David L. Swain laid the cornerstone on July 4, 1833, and the building was completed in 1840. At that time it housed all three branches of state government. Our founding fathers believed in culture as evidenced by the plans for our capitol building. The architect, David Paton, described the building, in the *North Carolina Manual*, as follows:

"The columns and entablature are Grecian Doric, and copied from the Temple of Minerva, commonly called the Parthenon, which was erected in Athens about 500 years before Christ. An octagon tower surrounds the rotunda, which is ornamented with Grecian cornices, etc., and its dome is decorated at top with similar ornament to that of the Choragic Monument of Lysicrated, commonly called the Lantorn of Demosthenes."

And further:

"The lobbies and hall of Representative have their columns and antae of the Octagon Tower of Andronicus Cyrrhestes and the plan of the hall is of the formation of the Greek theatre and of the Temple of Erectheus, Minerva Polias, and Pandrosus, in the Acropolis of Athens, near the above named Parthenon."

Not only were our forebears cultured, they were frugal. They housed all of government in one building. The executive branch on the first floor, the legislative branch on the second floor and the supreme court in the attic.

Mr. Paton's further description:

"The interior of the Capitol is divided into three stories: First, the lower story, consisting of ten rooms, eight of which are appropriated as offices to the Governor, Secretary, Treasurer, and Comptroller . . .

"The second story consists of Senatorial and Representatives' chambers, the former containing an area of 2,545 and the latter 2,849 square feet . . ."

(Since there were only 50 senators, but 120 representatives, the House was somewhat crowded.)

Our George Washington

In the rotunda of the original capitol was a statue of George Washington by a famous Italian sculptor. It depicted our first president wearing a Roman toga with a garland wreath on his head. This work of art was destroyed in the fire of 1831. Around 1960, North Carolina art lovers, led by Edwin Gill, the beloved state treasurer, conducted a campaign to raise the money to replace the statue. Gill was dismayed to discover that Representative Phil Godwin, a good friend, was opposed to the project. So one day Gill, a formidable man, waddled over to Godwin's office in the legislative building, and the following conversation took place:

Gill: Phillip, I understand you are against the statue of George Washington.

Godwin (bravely): Well, I am, Mr. Gill.

Gill: Would you please tell me why?

Godwin: Well, it costs a lot of money and it just don't look like George Washington.

Gill: Well, I will ask you one more question. When in hell did you ever see George Washington?

Gill and his many supporters won the day, and visitors today to the state capitol can decide for themselves whether the marble statue, centered in the rotunda, looks like George Washington.

The New Status Quo

In the 1950s, the General Assembly of North Carolina approved the construction of a new legislative building, which was located about five hundred yards north of the state capitol building. Most thought it was beautiful, but some didn't. One who didn't was Dr. Robert Lee Humber, a senator from Pitt County. How he got elected I'll never know because he lived in a world of art and history. While he was campaigning for office in a small country town, he stopped to talk with a local farmer, seeking support. After about thirty minutes he moved on, and several other farmers who were seated on a nearby bench asked the farmer whom he was talking with for so long. The farmer replied, "I ain't sure, but he sounded something like Socrates."

Doctor Humber did not believe in the new style of architecture. He preferred the original design of the capitol building. One night he and I were walking out of the new legislative building and I asked him what he thought about it. His answer was, "I guess it's all right, but if you were in Las Vegas it would just look like a new hotel."

ACHIEVEMENTS AND
CONTROVERSIES

Rules

The North Carolina Constitution states that "the General Assembly shall provide for the organization and government and the fixing of boundaries of counties, cities and towns, and other governmental subdivisions as it may deem advisable." Every county was established by a bill passed in the general assembly, as was every town. Most of our towns, which had existed without incorporation, became legal municipalities in the 1800s.

For example, in 1869 the general assembly passed this bill: "The Town of Wilkesboro is declared incorporated and its corporate limits shall be one-half mile in every direction beginning at the courthouse (this means it was circular) but not to cross the Yadkin River. The first election for Mayor, Commissioners and Constable shall be held within ninety days from the ratification of this act."

At the same legislative session, the mayors and commissioners of Robbinsville were given power to lay out and open streets and, if necessary, to condemn land for this purpose. Other incorporations in the same year included the Town of Mount Olive in Wayne County, Mount Airy in Surry County, the Town of Winston in Forsyth, Magnolia in Duplin, Smithfield in Johnston, Snow Hill in Greene, Joyner and Black Creek in Wilson, Bakersville in Mitchell and Greensboro in Guilford County.

Our state constitution not only gives the legislature the authority to provide for fixing the boundaries of counties, cities and towns, it also can give such powers and duties to them as it might deem advisable. Down through the years, the majority of bills passed by the legislature have applied only to particular counties or particular towns. When I first went to the legislature, one-half to three-quarters of all the bills passed were for this purpose. From time to time, efforts have been made to give local government what is known as "home rule" but these efforts have always been defeated. "Home rule" makes some sense. When Terry Sanford was governor, he advocated "home rule" without success. The status quo is a strong deterrent for change. First, it would substantially reduce the volume of legislative acts. Second, since the "one man, one vote" laws have come about, many counties are not directly represented in the general assembly, even though our forefathers provided that every county should have a representative and that representative could decide what was needed for his county. Third, there was an inviolate rule that if I represented Anson County and introduced a "local bill," it would pass 170-0, whether the other members thought it was a bad bill or not. The theory was that I should know what was good for my county, and even if I didn't, they certainly were not going to oppose it. If I was wrong, I wouldn't be back for the next session and my successor could repeal it.

Since the legislature controls local government, it might be worth considering letting every county that doesn't have a resident representative elect an honorary representative, without the power to vote, who could meet with the elected representative from his district and tell him or her how to vote on any issue that only affects his county. I'm sure the voting legislators would consider the request, and I feel equally sure the North Carolina Supreme Court could not find this to be unconstitutional.

Town commissioners or councils have limited authority given by the legislature to adopt ordinances designed to promote the welfare of its citizens. Many of these remind you of the Ten Commandments. In 1964, the town ordinances of Wadesboro contained the following:

It shall be unlawful for any person to sell, barter, or exchange any wine or beer . . . in any public place within the Town limits between Saturday at 11:45 P.M. to the following Monday at 7:30 A.M.

No person shall keep any cow, bull, or ox within the fire district or to stake the same within 200 feet of any dwelling house, church, stone building or any other public building.

The tying of horses or mules to any of the shade trees, electric light poles or fences of the Town, or to feed any of said animals on the street is forbidden.

No person shall be permitted to keep or maintain any hog pen, or keep any hogs within the corporate limits.

It shall be unlawful for any person to allow his bitch to run at large or to appear on any street or public place while in heat or in the erotic state of copulation. It shall be the duty of the police officers to kill every such bitch found running at large in this condition if its owner is unknown.

It shall be unlawful for any person to throw hulls, peelings or other litter upon any of the sidewalks or upon the floors of any church, public halls, theaters or other public places over which the public is accustomed to pass.

It shall be unlawful to beg unless a permit to do so has been obtained.

It shall be unlawful for any occupant of a disorderly house to refuse to give entrance to any policeman demanding admission for the purpose of suppressing disorderly conduct.

It shall be unlawful to shoot any gun or firearm except in the case of necessity.

It shall be unlawful for any person to loiter on the streets, or any public places beyond a reasonable time.

The operation of motion picture theaters on Sunday shall be at the pleasure of the County Commissioners between 2 P.M. and 4:15 P.M. and from 9:15 P.M.. until 11:30 P.M.

No person shall keep open for business any store or shop or sell any articles of merchandise on Sundays.

It shall be unlawful for all tramps, vagrants, or persons without any visible means of support to remain in the Town beyond a reasonable time.

It shall be unlawful to construct or repair any building, or outhouse, unless the building is rat proof.

Wadesboro has brought its ordinances up to date since 1964.

If the Supreme Court of the United States sat in Wadesboro, the justices would stay busy deciding the constitutionality of the town ordinances. As towns developed, they were akin to one happy family, which had rules as to what was proper conduct. It was a way of life and reflected what were the niceties of life and was socially proper for the time. To me, it wasn't so bad. Obviously the rules of the Christian church influenced and were made a part of the law. No store could open on Sunday, no alcoholic beverages could be sold and no picture show could be shown at a time that might conflict with a church service.

Boundaries have always been important markers in our history and growth. The North Carolina state boundaries were surveyed with the approval of South Carolina, Virginia, Georgia and Tennessee. They have never changed, although North Carolina almost had a war with Georgia over a boundary line in western North Carolina. Once set by the general assembly, the 100 county boundaries have not been changed.

On the subject of state lines, my friend, Phil Godwin, told me of an interesting event that occurred when the boundary between North Carolina and Virginia was being surveyed. The surveyors started on the coast in eastern North Carolina and headed west. When they got to the Great Dismal Swamp, the surveying became about impossible, so they said, "To hell with this. Let's get out of here and start again." So they went several miles south and started over and went all the way to Tennessee on the wrong line. If you look at an authentic map, you will see the indenture is still there. The Great Dismal Swamp cost North Carolina millions of acres of land, but having seen the Great Dismal Swamp, I can't blame the surveyors.

Freedom of Speech

The Thirteen Colonies would not agree to the proposed Constitution of the United States unless attached would be a Bill of Rights, the first right of which was this:

ARTICLE ONE: Congress shall make no law respecting an establishment of religion, or prohibiting the free exercise thereof, or abridging the freedom of speech or of the press, or the right of people peacefully to assemble and to petition the government for the redress of grievances.

Ironically, a provision that was so important in 1791 was never placed in the constitution of North Carolina until 1971, when by vote of the people this language was added:

Freedom of speech and of the press are two of the great bulwarks of liberty and therefore shall never be restrained, but every person shall be responsible for their abuse.

The constitution of the Confederacy also included a provision that guaranteed freedom of speech.

It should be pointed out that freedom of speech is not an absolute right. It is subject to certain restrictions. You cannot slander someone without being held responsible for doing so. You cannot yell "Fire" in a crowded theater. To do so has been held to be a crime. Vulgar language has been outlawed by statute and city ordinances for over 100 years.

In 1890, Laura Toole was convicted of walking down the streets of Charlotte singing in a loud and boisterous manner a song with several verses, one of which was considered to be obscene. The case went to the Supreme Court of North Carolina and the conviction was upheld on a theory that what she did was a public nuisance.

In 1914, Bessie Moore was convicted on evidence in the Town of Spencer that as she stepped into her buggy, a policeman cautioned her not to drive her horse and buggy through the main part of town, to which she replied that she would drive "where she damn pleased." She claimed her right to freedom of speech and appealed her case to the supreme court, which in effect reversed the case on the theory that only the policeman heard what she said and it therefore was not a public nuisance.

The supreme court, in its decision, very neatly avoided the question of vulgarity by saying, "We will not venture upon any casuistry [a doctrine of dealing with cases of conscience and the resolution of questions of right or wrong in conduct] discussion of the question of whether the word 'damn' is profanity or not, as the decision in the case does not demand it."

These brief ramblings about freedom of speech are a prelude to recalling two events that occurred in the General Assembly of North Carolina in 1925 and 1967, each of which created a maelstrom in the state that lasted for several years.

The Monkey Bill

In July 1925, a small town in Tennessee gained international focus when John Scopes, a biology teacher in the local high school, was tried for violating the state's anti-evolution law (*Preachers, Pedagogues and Politicians,* William B. Gatewood, Jr., 1966). Clarence Darrow, a famous criminal lawyer and confirmed agnostic, represented the defendant. William Jennings Bryan, equally famous as a lawyer and national political figure, spoke for the prosecution and delivered his ringing statement that America was as unwilling to be crucified on a cross of evolution as on a cross of gold. The case is still known as the Monkey Trial, based on the charge that evolutionists believed man descended from a monkey.

In the same year of Tennessee's Monkey Trial, North Carolinians fought over what its critics called the Monkey Bill. On January 8, 1925, the second day of the legislative session, Representative David Scott Poole, a part-time teacher and editor of *The Hoke County Journal*, introduced the following resolution:

> *Resolved by the House of Representatives, the Senate concurring, that it is the sense of the General Assembly of the State of*

North Carolina that it is injurious to the welfare of the people of the State of North Carolina for any official teacher in the State, paid wholly or in part by taxation, to teach or permit to be taught, as a fact either Darwinism or any other evolutionary hypothesis that links man in a blood relationship with any lower form of life.

Presbyterians, including Gov. Cameron Morrison, were solidly behind Poole's resolution. Among its prominent opponents was Dr. William Louis Poteat, the president of Wake Forest College, a Baptist institution. Dr. Poteat was also a professor of biology, a distinguished scholar noted for his broad range of interests, a tenacious defender of freedom of the mind, and a deeply religious Baptist. In the 1920s, he already had established a reputation as an outspoken and sometimes controversial defender of freedom of inquiry and speech.

But it was Harry W. Chase, president of the University of North Carolina, who assumed command of the opposition, despite warnings that his stand could adversely affect legislative appropriations to the university. He told Dr. Poteat, "You have fought our battles long enough, and now we are going to do some fighting ourselves."

Among legislative opponents of the resolution was young Representative Sam J. Ervin Jr. of Burke County, who later became a nationally known U.S. senator. Ervin said Poole's resolution "serves no good purpose except to absolve monkeys of their responsibility for the human race."

The resolution was defeated, but not before religious leaders, educators and editorial writers had their say on both sides of the issue. Here are some of their comments:

The monkey has replaced the donkey in Tar Heel Democracy.
—*The Greensboro Daily News*

If teachers of science use geology, biology and other sciences to unsettle the religious faith of our children, the Christian people of our country are not going to stand for it, and they ought not to stand for it.

—Governor Cameron Morrison

The Southerner is reared with a consciousness of the Bible. His religion historically has been subject to Calvinist and other fundamental doctrines. The Southerner is apt frequently to quote scripture and to have a fondness for the more articulate charlatans in religion as he has for his more preposterous rascally politicians.

—Ralph McGill, Atlanta editor

It is not a question of the truth or falsity of the evolution theory. This is a problem which each man is free to settle for himself. It is a question, however, of academic freedom and in the last analysis of religious freedom. It involves the whole issue of freedom of speech and conscience. Shall our teachers be free to follow the truth wherever it leads them or submit to political censorship.

—*The Asheville Times*

Some 40 years later, a similar controversy arose out of a legislative initiative that some saw as a threat to freedom and others saw as a defense of freedom: the Speaker Ban.

The Speaker Ban

It was the afternoon of the day before adjournment of the 1963 session of the General Assembly of North Carolina. Members of the House of Representatives and the Senate, weary from a long session, were plowing through full calendars of bills, disposing of them routinely. None was expected to cause any controversy. The big money bills, finance and appropriations, had already been put to bed. In the House, the well-respected Philip P. Godwin of Gates County rose from his seat and the following scenario took place:

Speaker: "For what purpose does the gentleman from Gates rise?"

Godwin: "To send forth a bill."

Whereupon he handed the bill to a page who carried it forward to the reading clerk who read: "An Act to regulate visiting speakers at state-supported colleges and universities."

Godwin (still standing): "Mr. Speaker, I move the rules be suspended and the bill be placed on the calendar for immediate passage. (This motion meant the bill would not go to committee as required by the House rules. See No. 1, below.)

Speaker: "All those in favor of the motion say 'aye,' those opposed 'no,' the 'ayes' seem to have it. The 'ayes' have it. The bill having passed its second reading will, without objection, be read a third time. Any debate? If not, all those who favor the passage of the bill on the third reading will say 'aye,' those opposed 'no.' The bill has passed its third reading and will be sent to the Senate." (See No. 2, below.)

Godwin: "Mr. Speaker, I move that the bill be sent to the Senate by special messenger." (This meant someone from the clerk's office would immediately carry it to the Senate, which was about one hundred feet away.)

The bill was carried to the Senate. The procedure used there was identical to that used in the House and the bill was ordered enrolled. In less than an hour, Phil Godwin's bill became law. Let me add two notes of explanation:

1. At the beginning of every session, the Speaker of the House appoints the committees and the chairman of each committee. It was a form of patronage because everyone wanted to be a chairman. There were some 45 committees, many of which never had a bill referred to it during the entire session. The chairman would have stationery printed showing his name as the chairman, and all legislators liked that. The two most important committees were Finance and Appropriations. One raised the money and the other spent it. Every member was appointed to one or the other committee. The Speaker would assign every bill introduced to a committee, whose responsibility was to have the sponsor explain it, then hear any witnesses, for or against the bill. Finally, the committee would vote to give the bill a favorable or unfavorable report, and send it back to the floor for a vote. If it was given an unfavorable report, it would take a two-thirds vote to put it on the calendar for a vote. I would guess that the Speaker Ban bill might have gotten on the calendar even it had gotten an unfavorable report.

It reminds me of the 1971 session, when a new constitution was being drafted to submit to a vote of the people of North Carolina. There was a provision in the old constitution that had been there for one hundred years, which read: "Beneficent provisions for the poor, the unfortunate, and orphan being one of a Christian State, the

General Assembly shall, at its first session, appoint and define the duties of a Board of Public Charities . . ." I thought in keeping with modern thinking that the word "Christian" should be replaced by something like "religious." I talked with the chairman of the committee about my thoughts. He replied, "Pat, I've voted for liquor twice in this session, and I'll be damned if I am going to vote against Christians." It is still in the constitution. I hope the U.S. Supreme Court doesn't hear about it. The legislature did take out a constitutional provision that stated: "It shall be the duty of the Legislature, as soon as practical, to devise means for the education of idiots and inebriates." Some people might have thought this was meant to apply to legislators.

2. When a bill is introduced, it is considered to be the first reading. After it goes to committee and comes back to the floor, it is voted on, and it passes; that is the second reading, and the normal process was to take the third and final vote immediately after the second vote. The constitution requires three readings, but not on separate days. There was one exception, and that related to a matter that was near and dear to our Founding Fathers, namely, taxes. They provided: "No law shall be passed to raise money on the credit of the State, or to pledge the faith of the State, directly or indirectly, for the payment of any debt, or to impose any tax upon the people of the State, or to allow the counties, cities or towns to do so unless the bill for the purpose shall have been read three several times in each house of the General Assembly and passed three several readings, which readings shall have been on three different days, and agreed to by each House respectively, and unless the 'yeas' and 'nays' on the second and third readings of the bill shall have been entered on the journal." The last provision was to prevent a legislator from saying he voted against a tax when the people back home would have a record that showed he voted for the tax.

Now that Phil Godwin's bill was law, what did it provide? Here is the text:

The General Assembly do enact:
Section I. No college or university which receives any state funds

and support thereof shall permit any person to use the facilities of such university for speaking purposes who:

a.   is a known member of the Communist Party.
b.   is known to advocate the overthrow of the Constitution of the United States or of the State of North Carolina.
c.   has pled the Fifth Amendment of the Constitution of the United States in refusing to answer any questions with respect to the Communist Party or subversive acts, connections or activities before any duly constituted legislative committee, any judicial tribunal, or any administrative board of trustees, or other governing authority of such college or university.

To some, on the face of it, the bill sounded rather innocuous. Overnight, however, it became apparent to some legislators how serious the implications of the law might be. Senator Hector McLean and others moved on the final day—June 26—to recall the bill from the enrolling office. When that motion failed, the following statement was placed in the *Senate Journal*: "We believe it (the bill) constitutes an abridgement or denial of free speech, a lack of due regard for the true meaning of the University of North Carolina and other public educational institutions, a denial of constitutional privileges and violates the long-established political and social principles of this country."

During the next two years, there was angry and heated controversy in higher education on this issue. It turned into an educational and political firestorm that engulfed all state-supported institutions of higher education, their administrators, trustees, members of the general assembly, and Governor Dan K. Moore, who inherited the crisis when he was inaugurated in January 1965.

There was a highly publicized threat that state universities would lose their accreditation. All of this resulted not by any action of the Communists, but by raising the question of academic freedom. As Speaker of the House in 1965-66, I also inherited the crisis.

If the citizens of North Carolina had been asked if they opposed Communism, 99 percent would have said yes and would have opposed allowing Communists to speak at their state universities.

Legislators are so sensitive to voter opinion that they would be inclined to vote for a ban not only of Communist speakers, but also of legislators who speak in favor of such a ban.

The Cold War was still the context of much national political debate. American soldiers were dying every day in a hot war in Vietnam. In both wars, cold and hot, the enemy was Communism. There is no question in my mind that if the Speaker Ban law had been put to a popular vote in North Carolina, it would have been approved overwhelmingly. But those who opposed it knew that the law, no matter how popular, struck at the very heart of fundamental principles of freedom of speech and academic freedom.

The sponsors of the legislation knew deep down that there would be a strong argument against it. That may be why they introduced the bill in the manner they did. But it should be understood that they were good Americans, good North Carolinians and thought they were trying to help the university.

The controversy continued during the entire 1965 session of the General Assembly. If you supported the law, you were charged with opposing freedom of speech and freedom of thought. If you were against it, you were a "communist." On the very last day of the Session, the General Assembly did what it does so often. If they can't solve the problem, they appoint a "study commision." In this instance, case members who served on the "commission" were good at compromise and it only took them a short period of time to come up with a solution. They put the responsibility for approving visiting speakers to our State universities on the Trustees and Administrators of each University. This was rapidly approved at a Special Session of the General Assembly.

A side issue at that Session related to me as Speaker and any political future I might have. Some of my close friends were concerned as to how I might vote on the issue and particularly if there was a tie vote. I told them not to worry because I could assure them that there would be no tie vote.

When there was a voice note, the Speaker would say, "All those in favor say 'Aye,'" followed by a chorus of "Ayes." Then, "All those who oppose the bill say 'No,'" followed by a chorus of "Noes." (As a rule, each voter would shout to make it sound like two votes.) At this point the Speaker would say, "The 'Ayes' (or 'Noes') seem to have it." He would then pause so that any member who thought the Speaker's hearing was bad could call out "Division," at which point the speaker would say, "All those in favor, please stand." At this point the Speaker, the Reading Clerk, and the Principal Clerk would each count votes. (I never told anyone this before, but while we almost always agreed, if we didn't, I took my count.) All of this is to illustrate that if the vote ended in a tie I could legitimately say the "Ayes" or the "Noes" had it, because as a member of the House I could vote and nothing in the rules said I had to announce my vote.

When I was Lieutenant Governor it was a little different. I was not a member of the fifty-man Senate and could only vote in case of a tie and the rules required that the Lieutenant Governor had to announce his vote. During my four year tenure there never was a tie vote!

In 1968 this whole war ended when a Federal Court declared the whole thing "unconstitutional." It all turned into "Much To Do About Nothing."

Since those days, the leaders of state-supported higher education and others have cited the Speaker Ban law as a tale of horror in which the forces of darkness almost overran the forces of free inquiry and the freedom to study, teach and publish. Most of these academic critics have never really understood how all this happened and how much they contributed to complicating and slowing down the final solution.

The sponsors of the Speaker Ban law and their legislative supporters believed the bill had merit and reflected their genuine concern about the threat of totalitarian aggression to our nation and to our young people. Many were tired of hearing professors on state payrolls running down the American system of government. The sponsors hoped that the whole experience had some long-term beneficial effect on the state-supported universities, and how they schedule outside speakers. What if Hitler had been invited to speak at UNC-Chapel Hill in 1944?

The record-breaking passage of the Speaker Ban Law was a learning experience for many members of the General Assembly, and others who cherish its safeguards of checks and balances. The passage was a classic example of how sponsors of a bill can circumvent the normal, orderly process of the legislature. Only experienced legislators or others close to the process understand how this is done.

It is important to understand the dilemma that members of the General Assembly of North Carolina or any other legislative body often face as they carry out their responsibilities. You have to vote yes or no, but you may in fact think the bill is 47 percent good and 53 percent bad. If you vote yes people believe that means you think the bill is 100 percent good.

I think the best people in public service are those who recognize that there is something good to be said and something bad to be said about most legislation, especially on issues of some importance. Controversial legislation is almost always amended many times before passage. But if you speak of this dilemma in public, you are called a fence straddler. And nobody likes a fence straddler.

Since Phil Godwin was the author of the Speaker Ban bill, I asked him to comment on this account of the controversy. Here is Godwin's response in a letter written to me February 26, 2001. (Godwin died in September 2001.):

> . . . *Basically, your facts that are related are correct; however, there is one thing that the press and many opponents will not for some reason realize and accept and that is that this matter came about on the spur of the moment and was not born in a dark smoke-filled hotel room with bourbon flowing and the stars and stripes playing on the radio. There was no sinister background or reason or "out to get you" thinking at the time that this bill was introduced.*
>
> *I have related on television and in the press the reason that I gave birth to the idea, but my reason is too simple and is not involved in mysterious political misbehavior; therefore, it has not been accepted, but I can tell you honestly and God is my witness that*

the whole idea came about because of a young man's death in my county [Gates] who was serving in Vietnam, enlisted and was killed in less than eight months. I did not know him personally, but I did know his father and mother. This tragedy preyed on my mind and soul with the question arising, "What did this young man give his life for?"

I served in World War II in the South Pacific as a member of the 5th Air Force and I really believed that from the time I took my oath as a soldier that I had a purpose for being in the uniform and after Pearl Harbor I was convinced that I had a purpose, and history has proven that all of those who served and those who gave their life had a purpose.

The only answer that I could ever get in my inquiry as to why Ivan Bunch gave his life was that his life had to be given to stop the spread of Communism and I have always believed that our involvement in that part of the world was more political than it was in defense of this country. I reasoned with myself and sought the advice of others to the end that if we were willing to sacrifice our sons to stop the spread of Communism, why not show some good intent to stop it here at home; not under the flag of Senator McCarthy, but through legislation that would let our state-supported institutions realize that we did not want the Communists peddling their wares and using our state institutions as a forum.

I did not try to take advantage of Speaker Blue or the legislature in the timing of the introduction of the bill. I had discussed the bill with Ned Delamar and he advised me that he would have the bill drafted if I would introduce it and that is what happened. I would be less than honest if I did not say that once the bill was introduced I realized that I had to move forward and that someone had struck a match to the political firestorm and the rest of the story is for the historians.

There is one thing that must be remembered. This bill and law had much more support throughout this state than the press would ever admit.

JUSTICE

Court Reform

In 1955, my first year in the legislature, the judicial system of North Carolina had supreme court justices, seven I believe, some 30 odd superior court judges, some 100 county court judges, but we had, I would guess, 5,000 justices of the peace, maybe more. Avery Hightower was our state senator, and he and I appointed 38 justices of the peace for Anson County. That's more judges than Governor Hunt appointed in eight years.

Justices of the Peace, also called squires, and sometimes judges, while selected by their legislators, were actually appointed by the General Assembly. A historical position, it amounted to a court for rural areas so that people did not have to travel to the county courthouse to file a complaint or take out a warrant. One great advantage of it was its peacemaking function. The scenario, in many cases, would go like this: Farmer Jones would come to the justice of the peace and want to sue or take out a warrant against Farmer Smith, his neighbor. The justice would say, "I would like to talk with Bill Smith and see if I can't get this problem straightened out," and very often he could. That is where the word "peace" came into play. If he couldn't, court would be held at his home or a country store.

A lot of people wanted to be a justice of the peace for the prestige of being called judge or squire, and since there was no salary for the office, you tended to have only respectable persons asking their legislators to appoint them. In some circumstances, justices were compensated, however, and that method of compensation was to have a profound effect on the judicial system of North Carolina.

Luther H. Hodges, the Lieutenant Governor, became governor because of the sudden death of Governor William B. Umstead in 1954. Hodges had been a very successful businessman, but he was in his first term of public office and he had little knowledge of the state judicial system. By chance, he learned that in a criminal case a justice of the peace received no compensation unless he found the defendant guilty. It could be compared to telling juries they would not be paid if they found the defendant innocent, but would be paid if they found him guilty. This shocked the new governor and he appointed a blue ribbon commission, headed by a prominent Charlotte lawyer, Spencer Bell, and as a result, the lowly justice of the peace was responsible for a total change in the North Carolina court system.

After an extensive study, the Bell commission made a report to the 1959 session of the legislature, recommending a totally new system along the lines of the system that England had adopted 100 years before. Among the provisions, it did away with justices of the peace and replaced them with magistrates, who would be part of a one court system. Now it is necessary for the farmer to travel to the courthouse to take out a warrant or to sue for debt claims or property damage. Court is no longer held in a country store close to home. Those who opposed the Bell Plan had a justifiable complaint.

The Bell Plan also provided that all judges would be appointed, not elected. This incurred the wrath of the well-loved state treasurer, Edwin Gill, who traveled around the state preaching the dangers he saw if the people did not elect judges. Mr. Gill was a historian, and to reinforce his point he warned of corrupt judges going back to Julius Caesar.

Senator Bell was very intelligent, somewhat pompous, and did not understand the word "compromise." A great North Carolinian,

Lindsay Warren, who, in his later years, was a state senator, opposed certain provisions of the proposed Bell Plan, as did many others, which led to its defeat in 1959. Since the Bell Plan involved amending the state constitution, three-fifths of the members of both houses had to approve the proposal, and then it had to be approved by the voters of North Carolina in a general election.

The plan failed in 1959, but was approved by the 1961 General Assembly. It was necessary, however, to delete the provision relating to the election of judges. I was chairman of the House committee that considered the Bell Plan and can verify that it would not have passed without the assistance of Gus Zollicoffer, Dick Phillips, Buck Harris and Jim McMillan, who at the time was president of the North Carolina Bar Association.

Today, the method of election of judges is of serious concern in this country. It is pretty well accepted that popular election is not a good way to do it. In political campaigns for other offices, voters can base their choices on candidates' positions on issues, on their perception of candidates' character, intelligence and common sense, and on candidates' records of achievement in both public and private life, and those are meaningful criteria for a legislative or executive office. But judges don't make decisions on issues. They rule on cases, based on the requirements of law. To be a good judge requires not only intelligence and common sense, but also extensive knowledge of the law and legal precedents and interpretations. Candidates for the judiciary can't promise to build roads or create jobs or cut taxes. So it is much more difficult for voters to make informed choices in judicial elections than in, say, legislative elections.

Several years ago a layman with no judicial background came close to being elected to the Supreme Court of North Carolina, which dramatized the need for selecting judges by some method of appointment, not by elections. But who gets to make the appointments? That's the question that gets politics into the equation. Democrats don't want a Republican to make the appointments and vice versa.

In North Carolina today, supreme court and superior court judges are elected. District court judges are appointed by the governor, with one proviso: the district bar of the judicial district from which the new judge is to be selected submits three candidates to the governor and rates them number one, number two and number three. Several years ago, our district submitted three names to Governor Hunt and he appointed number three. There was a strong feeling that politics motivated the appointment.

U.S. Supreme Court justices and federal judges are appointed for life with the hope they will not have to worry about public opinion and running for reelection. The Constitution went so far as to say that their salary could not be reduced from its initial level. They are appointed by the President and the United States Senate must confirm the appointment. Here again, the nominee is appointed by a politician who believes his choice adheres to his political philosophy. Meanwhile, justices of the peace are gone and all judges are state employees.

The most recent proposal is to have judges appointed by an independent and impartial commission. Who is going to appoint the commission?

Juries

Until the court reform in North Carolina in 1961, the court system was structured such that the state had a supreme court and superior courts. Less serious cases were the responsibility of the counties and there were county courts and justices of the peace. Justices of the peace were laymen and some county court judges were not lawyers.

In county court in Anson County, a defendant could request a six-man jury trial. Since our state constitution guaranteed a 12-man jury, if the defendant lost his case before the six-man jury he could appeal to superior court and get a 12-man jury trial. Most of the time if the defendant lost before six jurors, he would decide that was enough, particularly if the sentence was not too severe. Superior court judges had the reputation of being more severe and would more often send the defendant to prison.

I use the term six-man jury and 12-man jury because only white males served on the jury. Women and blacks were excluded. That's where the phrase "gentlemen of the jury" came from.

On one occasion, I represented a fine old black man on a charge of driving drunk. He came from Gulledge Township and I had five of our best citizens, three blacks and two whites, to testify to his good character. The jury retired and returned the following verdict: "We find the defendant to be a fine nigger, but we think he is guilty." I argued to the judge that he should find my client innocent because the law requires a unanimous finding that the defendant is guilty beyond a reasonable doubt. Judge Calligan, who was a newspaperman, was impressed, but turned to the jury and asked what they thought he should do. They unanimously said, "Let him go." And the judge did.

Capital Punishment

Capital punishment is as old as history. The earliest forms of capital punishment involved torture, as is evident in the manner in which Jesus Christ was executed. Even the most civilized countries in the last five hundred years made torture a part of executions. Such torture included drawing, quartering, burning at the stake, cutting off noses, arms or limbs, starving to death, or such as were inflicted by the act of the English Parliament during the reign of Henry VIII, which included having the prisoner poisoned or thrown into boiling water and boiled to death.

Capital punishment was established in North Carolina when the colonists came over to this country from England and the British Isles. They brought with them the criminal laws as they were there in force. The lord proprietors, in their first charter, were authorized "in person or by their deputies to make law . . . by imposition of penalties, imprisonment, or any other punishments, yea, if it be needful and the quality of the offense requires it, by taking away member and life."

The extent to which the colonists used this authority can be illustrated by a trial and punishment that occurred in Duplin County, eleven years after the Declaration of Independence and at the time the

Constitution of the United States was being written. On March 15, 1787, a trial was held at the courthouse in Duplin County, for Darby and Peter, two Negro slaves, the property of the late William Taylor, Esq. They were tried for the murder of their master. They were tried without the solemnity of jury but by three justices and four freeholders who were owners of slaves. The verdict of the court was:

> *The said Negro man, Darby, being brought before the Court, did confess that he did on the 13th day of this month feloniously and maliciously murder his master by striking him on the head with an axe into his brain of which his master instantly died. Whereupon the Court doth pass this sentence that the Negro man Darby be immediately committed under guard and that tomorrow between the hours of one and four o'clock in the afternoon he be taken out hence and tied to a stake on the Court House lot and there burned to death and his ashes strewn upon the ground. (Capital Punishment in North Carolina, 1929)*

Peter, a boy of about 14 years of age, was brought before the court and confessed that he was present when his master was murdered and that he did aid and assist Darby in committing the crime. The court, taking into consideration the youth of Peter and considering him to be under the influence of his older brother, thought it proper to pass this sentence:

> *That the said Negro boy, Peter, be committed to the jail and remain under good guard till tomorrow and between one and four o'clock he be taken thence and tied to a post on the Court House lot, and there to have one half of each ear cut off and that he be branded on each cheek with the letter M and receive one hundred lashes well laid on his bare back and that the Sheriff see this order executed. (Capital Punishment in North Carolina, 1929)*

In New Hanover County in 1768, a Negro slave convicted of robbery was beheaded and his head affixed upon the point near Wilmington.

I would suspect that it was these forms of punishment that led to the insertion in the Bill of Rights to the U.S. Constitution which reads: "Amendment VIII. Excessive bail shall not be required, nor excessive fine imposed, no cruel or unusual punishments inflicted."

In 1836, the following crimes were punishable by death without benefit of clergy in North Carolina: murder, burglary, arson, highway robbery, fighting a duel in which one of the parties was killed, castration, rape, crime against nature, house breaking in daylight when goods amounting to $2 were stolen, malicious maiming (second offense), breaking prison (when the person was imprisoned for a capital crime), a slave's embezzlement of his master's goods to the value of $10, stealing slaves, conveying free slaves out of state to sell them, circulating seditious literature calculated to incite slaves to insurrection, and inciting slaves to insurrection by word of mouth (second offense). Though killing a slave was murder and punishable by death, escaped slaves were outlawed and might be killed without penalty when public proclamation had been issued against them. Horse stealing had been a capital crime for well over 100 years.

The state constitution of 1868 limited capital punishment to four crimes: murder, rape, arson and burglary in the first degree. Also in 1868, a law was enacted that outlawed public executions and ordered that they should be held in the jail yard enclosure and as much removed from public as the means within the control of the sheriff would allow. Despite this provision for privacy, executions by hanging continued to be public in North Carolina until 1879. Today we still have the privacy provision in the law.

The law today relating to private executions reads:

At such executions there shall be present the warden or deputy warden . . . the surgeon or physician of the penitentiary and six respectable citizens; the counsel and any relations of such person, and a minister or ministers of the Gospel may be present if they so desire and the Board of Direction of the penitentiary may provide for and pay the fee for each execution not to exceed thirty-five dollars. (General Statutes of North Carolina)

Hanging remained the form of execution until 1909. The last hanging took place in Elizabethtown at high noon when

Henry Spivey, a black man, paid the death penalty for the murder of his father-in-law. In 1909, the method of inflicting the death penalty was changed by the legislature to electrocution and the first execution using the electric chair took place on March 18, 1910. Walter Morrison, a 37-year-old Negro of Robeson County, had been convicted of rape on Polly Rogers, a Croatan woman.

Subsequently, in 1935, the legislature substituted lethal gas for the electric chair and today the prisoner has a choice. The law reads: "If any person so chooses, he may at least five days prior to the execution date, elect in writing to be executed by the administration of a lethal quantity of ultra short-acting barbiturate in combination with a chemical paralytic agent." (*General Statutes of North Carolina*)

In the 1950s, the Supreme Court of the United States decided that the procedures followed in North Carolina in death penalty cases were inadequate and for over twenty years there were no executions in the state.

When I was elected to the legislature, I was opposed to capital punishment. My good friend Rep. W.C. (Buck) Harris (D-Wake) would introduce a bill to do away with capital punishment, and I would sign it as a co-sponsor. As I recollect, we would be the only two members of the House of Representatives to vote for the bill.

In my opinion, we are not far from abolishing capital punishment in this country. In 200 years, we have moved from imposing the death penalty for some twenty offenses down to just one: first-degree murder. We have moved from burning people at the stake, to hanging, to electrocution, to lethal gas, to lethal injection and from public to private executions. We take 10 to 20 years between conviction and execution. It all adds up to what I believe is a subconscious feeling that the deliberate taking of a human life is wrong. It is an eye for an eye and a tooth for a tooth philosophy. I am not sure that mankind has a right to take a human life using this philosophy.

I never heard my father say he was opposed to capital punishment and he probably was not, but in the 1920s he was appointed to represent Jim Collins in Anson County on a murder charge and I know that ever after he felt that Jim should not have been executed. The story of this case is taken from a *Bulletin on Capital Punishment in North Carolina* issued by the N.C. State Board of Charities and Public Welfare, and quoted verbatim below from *The News and Observer* of Raleigh and *The Greensboro Daily News*.

> *Jim Collins, 19-year-old Anson County Negro, who yesterday paid the death penalty in the electric chair at State's Prison, faced his doom with a calmness seldom achieved by the most heroic of men.*
>
> *"Howdy, you all," said Collins, in the best of humor, as he walked into the small chamber, accompanied by Rev. W.S. Shacklette, the prison chaplain, and three ministers of his own race.*
>
> *Repeating in a firm and clear voice the familiar strains of the Psalm beginning "The Lord is my Shepherd, I shall not want," the little Negro said at the end "All right." Chaplain Shacklette leaned over and shook the one hand that had been left by those who pursued the Negro for eight days, the straps were fastened and the current turned on.*
>
> *To all outward appearances the single shock was sufficient but Warden Norman, after one glance with an experienced eye, signaled for the current again and it was applied for the second time. Beyond the inevitable recoil from the shock of 1,800 volts of electricity, there was no sign from the body except a bright flare of flame and the odor of burning flesh. He went confidently to his doom and quietly he endured it.*
>
> *Collins was executed for shooting A.C. Sedberry, a white man weighing 215 pounds and a member of a prominent family. The shooting followed a quarrel precipitated by the white man, who assaulted the Negro and cuffed him about the head. The case has attracted little attention outside of Anson County, where the shooting provoked intense excitement last July and where interest has been maintained.*
>
> *Relatives and friends of Sedberry have worked unceasingly to see that the death penalty was imposed and attorneys for the private prosecution remained in the case through the hearing for clemency*

before Governor McLean. Collins, poor and friendless and without lawyers of his own, elicited the sympathy of the lawyers appointed by the Court to defend him, and their efforts received support from such disinterested persons as Assistant Attorney General Frank Nash and Bishop Joseph Blount Cheshire.

As the little Negro, who had already lost his right arm while fleeing from a mob, was led into the chamber to be strapped into the chair, J. Chesley Sedberry, Rockingham lawyer and brother of the man killed by Collins, pressed forward against the chain which shuts off a small space around the chair. The lawyer brother, who has followed the case all the way through the trial to the Superior Court, the appeal in the Supreme Court and the hearing for clemency before Governor McLean, missed no scintilla of what occurred yesterday.

After the dying declaration by the Negro youth, the brother of the dead man stepped back to the side of Baxter McRae, an eye witness to the killing, and remained near the wall of the little octagonal room, with his eyes glued upon the huddled form in the chair until two full shocks had been administered and Dr. J.H. Norman, prison warden and physician, had applied instruments to the shrunken form and had declared that all life was extinct.

The spectacle appeared to in no way affect the attitude of the brother. He stepped briskly into the conversation as one of the Negro ministers was relating to newspapermen the dead Negro's feeling of justification and declared the beating administered the Negro by his brother had been greatly exaggerated and that Collins was only slapped.

H.H. McLendon and H.P. Taylor, the attorneys appointed by the Court to defend the Negro, appealed to the Supreme Court on the theory that the evidence did not justify a first degree verdict. The Court kept the case from the fall term to the spring term but finally affirmed the judgment of the court below.

The case was brought before the Governor, with Assistant Attorney General Nash who argued the case on behalf of the state in the Supreme Court, asserting that the execution, under the circum-

stances, would be "an outrage to the state." Bishop Cheshire and others who ordinarily do not take part in such matters joined in and considerable effort was made to save the Negro. These efforts kept up through Thursday when the three Negro ministers who were with Collins in his last moments wired the Governor in New York.

Collins shot Sedberry on July 19, 1924. It was in evidence that he had made arrangements to give himself up but a mob formed before the Sheriff reached him and the Negro fled, being captured eight days later near the line between Stanly and Cabarrus counties.

After being cuffed by the white man, Collins got a shotgun, which was taken away from him, and then got a pistol, following Sedberry down the road and shooting him in the back. In the opinion of Supreme Court Justice Adams, [he] sets forth the circumstances of the killing as follows:

Sedberry: "Jim, why did you do like you did this morning?"

Collins: "Did what?"

Sedberry: "Send Oscar Culledge for the money."

Collins: "I just sent him."

Sedberry: "Ain't you a man of your own?"

Collins: "I am."

Sedberry: "Why did you not come and get it?"

Collins: "I just didn't come."

Sedberry: "I owe you $2.37 and carried you one night to see the doctor, didn't I?"

Collins: "You did."

Sedberry: "I didn't intend to charge you for that if you had stayed your time out you hired to work, but as you did not I am going to charge you $2.50 for that trip; that leaves you owing me 13 cents and I am going to strike off even with you."

Collins: "I don't give a damn what you do with it."

Sedberry (after stepping down from the road machine): "Don't you cuss me."

Collins: "I didn't cuss you."

Sedberry: "You cussed at me."

As Justice Adams reviewed the testimony, this conversation was *followed by a fight in which the white man jumped on the Negro and beat him up badly. The Negro got a shotgun and started after the white man, but the shotgun was taken away from him by another Negro. He then went and got a pistol with which he did the killing. (The News and Observer, The Greensboro Daily News.)*

The U.S. Supreme Court ruled in 2002 that it was cruel and unusual punishment and therefore unconstitutional to execute a person who is mentally retarded. This is one other step in the saga leading to the abolishment of the practice of taking a human life. "Thou shall not kill." The fifty states are reviewing their capital cases to comply with this decision.

According to a publication, *Capital Punishment in North Carolina,* prepared by the N.C. State Board of Charities and Public Welfare in 1929, the U.S. Supreme Court decision came much too late for at least four North Carolina prisoners. The following were tried, sentenced and electrocuted:

A 26-year-old Negro from Williamston, N.C., who had a mental age of eight years and an I.Q. of 50.

A 33-year-old Negro from Wilson, N.C., who had a mental age of five years, six months and an I.Q. of 34.

A 23-year-old Negro from Abbeville, S.C., who had a mental age of four years, six months and an I.Q. of 28.

A 24-year-old Negro from Americus, Georgia, who had a mental age of four years, ten months and an IQ of 30.

Up Close and Personal

When Ed Rankin joined the news staff of *The News and Observer* in Raleigh in 1941, he was assigned, among other tasks, to cover all executions at Central Prison in Raleigh. It was an *N&O* tradition: the newest reporter hired gets the least desirable assignments. Here, in his words, is his experience with a condemned prisoner and the governor who did not intervene:

> During my first days at *The News and Observer,* the city editor informed me that an execution was scheduled the next week. They were always held on a Friday morning at Central Prison, and usually received a routine eight or ten paragraph story inside the paper. There had been five executions that year. As a young, ambitious newcomer to the staff, I thought I could find a new angle and get a better story.
>
> From the court and prison records I found that the condemned man was a white male in his early forties, sentenced from Durham County, and that he had brutally murdered his wife in a drunken rage by striking her with an axe. I can't recall his name and will call him Hubert. When I called the warden at Central Prison and asked for an interview with Hubert, the warden said,

"Well, if it is okay with him, it's okay with me. I'll ask him." Hubert agreed to see me and the interview was set for Thursday morning before the Friday execution date.

It was my first visit to Central Prison, that massive collection of buildings, cellblocks, walls, fences, guard towers, floodlights and parking areas near downtown Raleigh. After meeting the warden, I was escorted to a room near Death Row overlooking the large exercise yard enclosed by a high brick and masonry wall. In a few minutes, Hubert was brought in by two guards (now called correction officers) who stationed themselves outside the closed door. A man of medium height and weight, with a very pale skin and balding head, Hubert wore blue denim pants, shirt, work shoes and was not handcuffed or shackled.

Hubert had a firm handshake and a quiet manner. We took seats near a window and watched an inmate baseball game underway in the yard below. I found that he was a baseball fan, followed the Yankees and we chatted about the current baseball season underway. Sensing my unease in asking about his case and impending fate, he told me briefly about his life as a factory worker in Durham and his marriage.

"I got to drinking too much," Hubert said, sadly, "and couldn't handle it, I guess. Things went from bad to worse. I didn't mean to hurt my wife—but I did. And I got to pay for it now."

We said goodbye and he thanked me for the visit. Returning to the warden's office, I learned that the prison chaplain would hold a worship service on Death Row that evening, and I persuaded the warden to slip me into an end cell just before the service began.

The Death Row tiers of cells faced an open dayroom area on the first floor and an exterior wall with many windows. A steel catwalk attached to the exterior wall enabled guards to stand there and see all the cells at a glance. The chaplain, an Episcopal priest, used this catwalk as his pulpit.

It was a Protestant service with prayers, scripture reading of familiar passages, and the singing of several well-known hymns.

Each Death Row inmate stood at his cell door looking out at the chaplain on the catwalk. The inmates could not see each other. I stood at my cell door, listened like they did, and joined in the singing and prayers.

The chaplain's message was filled with warm words of encouragement, faith and love of God and fellow man. Then he referred to Hubert, his fate, and asked the inmates for any words they wished to say. There was silence at first, and then a husky voice, "We are thinking of you, Hubert," and then another, "God bless you, Hubert," and another, "Hubert, it was good to know you," until almost all had chimed in.

The chaplain told Hubert that he would be with him each step of the way, and asked for anything Hubert wanted to say. There was a pause. Then Hubert's voice: "Well, the governor is gonna let me go down. I guess I'm as ready as I can be. I wish you all better luck."

On Friday morning I was one of the eight official witnesses standing next to the glass window looking at the empty chair with its high back, heavy oak construction, thick leather straps and square metal tank under the seat. It had been converted from electricity to lethal gas.

The heavy metal, airtight door opened on the other side of the octagonal death chamber and the warden, physician, chaplain, guards and Hubert walked in. As soon as Hubert was seated, the guards quickly strapped his legs, arms and chest to the chair. A black stethoscope was attached to his chest. Just before they lowered a black hood over his head, Hubert saw me, nodded and his lips moved to form the words, "Goodbye, Ed." I was frozen in place.

The chaplain placed his hands on the hooded head, said a prayer not heard by the witnesses, and the group filed out of the chamber. The door closed and the warden and others could be seen through a large glass window looking in at the figure in the chair. The warden nodded to someone and there was a sharp sound, "clack," as the device under the chair opened and released the poison pills into the tank of acid.

A gray vapor quickly rose from the tank and flowed over Hubert and into the chamber. He was startled at the sound and twisted his head up as far as he could under the hood restraints. As he breathed the gas, his pale white skin began to turn pink and then a fiery red. In a few minutes, which seemed forever, his head slumped forward and he appeared unconscious. After 18 minutes, the physician announced that Hubert was dead.

I could not even consider eating lunch after such an experience, so I returned to the N&O and wrote my story. It covered everything—my interview with Hubert, his last worship service on Death Row, the comments of his fellow inmates, his last words, and a graphic account of his death by lethal gas. To my surprise, the city editor liked the story so much he gave it good play on the front page.

My joy was cut short by a call the next afternoon from Tom Banks, private secretary to Governor J. Melville Broughton. "The Governor wants to see you," Banks said briskly. It did not occur to me to ask why. I immediately assumed it was about my story on Hubert. What facts did I have wrong? Banks gave me an appointment later that afternoon.

It was my first visit to the Governor's Office in the Capitol. And it was my first meeting with the governor. A large, avuncular man, the governor greeted me politely and took his seat behind an imposing desk. He came straight to the point. "I read your story on Hubert," he said, "and you have no idea how difficult it is for me, or any governor, to make decisions on death cases." I braced myself for the errors I must have made.

"It is true that I did not choose to intervene in Hubert's case," the governor continued, "but Hubert was put to death by order of a North Carolina court, not by an order of this North Carolina governor. I can understand his last words about me 'letting him go down,' but it does not make my life or decisions any easier. For your readers, it was a good story. But not for me. I just wanted you to hear my side of this case."

I thanked Governor Broughton for his comments, and returned to my office greatly relieved. When I told the city editor of my visit, he laughed and assured me that the governor's comments were proof that my story deserved front-page play. Governors, as elected officials, must take the bitter with the sweet, he said.

Capital Punishment, Western Style

The following is a verbatim transcript of a sentence imposed upon a defendant convicted of murder in the Federal District Court of the Territory of New Mexico in 1881 by a United States judge, sitting in Taos in an adobe stable used as a temporary courtroom:

Jose Manuel Miguel Xaviar Gonzales, in a few weeks it will be spring. The snows of winter will flee away, the ice will vanish, and the air will become soft and balmy. In short, Jose Manuel Miguel Xaviar Gonzales, the annual miracle of the years will awaken and come to pass, but you won't be there.

From every treetop some wild woods songster will carol his mating song, butterflies will sport in the sunshine, the busy bee will hum happy as it pursues its accustomed vocation, the gentle breeze will tease the tassels of the wild grasses, and all nature, Jose Manuel Miguel Xaviar Gonzales, will be happy but you. You won't be here to enjoy it because I command the Sheriff or some other officers of the country to lead you out to some remote spot, swing you by the neck from a knotting bough of some sturdy oak, and let you hang until you are dead.

And then, Jose Manuel Miguel Xaviar Gonzales, I further command that such officer or officers retire quickly from your dangling corpse (so) that vultures may descend from the heavens upon your filthy body until nothing shall remain but bare, bleached bones of a cold-blooded, copper-colored, blood thirsty, throatcutting, chili-eating, sheep-herding, murdering son-of-a-bitch. (United States of America v. Gonzales, United States District Court, New Mexico Territory Sessions, 1881.)

What About Real Bad People?

Old Bill and me went fishing one Sunday afternoon and got to talking about one thing and another. Finally, I said, "I don't care what they say. Killing somebody ain't good and it ain't right. Everybody has a mother and killing one of her children is a bad thing."

Old Bill said, "Well, some people are bad. I mean real bad."

I said, "I know you're right about that, but ain't everybody bad at sometime or another? At church this morning, the preacher said we're supposed to forgive everybody, don't matter how bad they are. To tell the truth, he says that about every Sunday, and he says God told him that, and if he ain't lying we're supposed to do what God says."

Old Bill said, "Well what in the hell are we going to do with 'em if you don't kill 'em? I don't want them running around and about doing bad things all the time."

I had to agree with that, so I said, "What about locking them up and keeping them locked up?"

Bill said, "That costs a lot of money 'cause you got to feed them and pay folks to watch 'em all the time. Some of 'em ain't worth feeding."

I didn't say nothing 'cause about everything Bill said made sense to me. So I said, "How about sending them to South Carolina?"

Bill agreed that there was something to that but said they'd come right back, "And remember the preacher said don't do nothing to somebody you wouldn't want done to you."

I started to say them folks in South Carolina like bad folks, but I didn't.

Well, Old Bill had me in a corner, but I finally thought up something pretty good and I said, "How about sending them to the jungles of Africa and if they want to kill something they can try out on lions and elephants? They'd have a hell of a time getting back."

And then I said, "A long time ago some white folks captured some black folks in Africa and brought them over here, and them black folks didn't want to come and were treated mighty bad when they got here."

Old Bill looked at me and says, "What's that got to do with what we are talking about?"

The only thing I could think of was that the preacher said everyone ought to be a fisherman. So we went back to fishing.

Georgia Justice

About fifty years ago Gene Talmadge was governor of Georgia and he gained a national reputation for being tough, particularly with blacks and criminals. A prisoner escaped from a Georgia chain gang, went to New Jersey and wrote a book entitled, *The Horrors of the Georgia Chain Gang*. It became a best seller and the governor of New Jersey received thousands of letters from people around the country begging the governor not to extradite the escaped prisoner back to Georgia because he had said in the book that if they ever got him back they would kill him

While the governor was trying to decide what to do, he received a telegram from Governor Talmadge reading: "If you don't have that prisoner in Georgia by next Saturday, I am going to parole one hundred of the most hardened criminals in the Georgia prisons on the condition that they move to New Jersey."

As I remember, he got his man back.

Supreme Court Politicians

Several years ago most of the members of the North Carolina Supreme Court were standing for reelection. They traveled around the State en banc. They asked me if I would take them around Wadesboro, which I was glad to do. When they were introduced one Justice said, "I would appreciate your support. If there is anything I can do for you, just let me know." I believe the Lord forgave them "for they knew not what they said." Most had been appointed and had little knowledge of how to campaign.

I can envision a defendant, who had been sentenced to be executed on a murder charge and his case was appealed to the Supreme Court, saying to the Court, "When ya'll were in Wadesboro you asked me to vote for you and you said, 'If there is anything I can do for you, just let me know.'"

Pride in North Carolina

Congressman from Pennsylvania:

Mr. Speaker, I have a question I would like to direct to the gentleman from North Carolina who was just speaking for the agricultural people in the country. I would like for him to tell me whether this statement is correct or not.

The North Carolina farmer gets up in the morning to the alarm of a Connecticut clock, buttons his Chicago suspenders to Detroit overalls, washes his face with Cincinnati soap in a Pennsylvania pan, sits down to a Grand Rapids table, eats his Chicago meat, sprinkled with Tennessee flour cooked with Kansas lard on a St. Louis stove. He puts a New York bridle on a Kansas mule fed with Iowa corn. He plows a farm covered by an Ohio mortgage, with a Chattanooga plow. At the end of the day he says a prayer written in Jerusalem, crawls under a blanket made in New Hampshire, only to be kept awake by a North Carolina hound dog that howls all night, the only home product on the place.

Answer:

Mr. Speaker, the people of Pennsylvania should love North

Carolina because we are among the best customers of the industrial state of Pennsylvania. But when the gentleman speaks disparagingly of a North Carolina hound dog, he has gone too far. Mr. Speaker, if all the cows in North Carolina were one cow, she could stand with her front feet in the great plains of the West, her hind feet in the dominion of Canada, and with her mighty tail, could swirl the icicles off the North Pole. If all the hogs in North Carolina were one hog, he could stand with his front feet in the Caribbean, his hind feet in the Atlantic Ocean, and with his tremendous snout could dig another Panama Canal. And if all the dogs in North Carolina were one dog, he could stand on the top of Mt. Mitchell and raise a howl that would blow the rings off the planet Saturn—not all the groundhogs in Pennsylvania could cast a shadow across his left hind leg.

This is somewhat inconsistent with the old saying: "North Carolina is a valley of humility between two mountains of conceit." (Virginia and South Carolina)

How North Carolina Prevented an Ammendment to the U.S. Constitution

In 1901 an article appeared in *Independist* by Henry T. Finch, which began:

One of the most important problems to be resolved in the new century is this: shall women be flowers or vegetables, ornamental or useful? In other words, shall women work, and if so, what shall their work be and where shall it be . . .in the garden attached to the home or in the field at large?

A considerable number of agitators are trying hard to persuade women that it is their duty to make themselves independent and self-supporting, not only potentially but actually . . . their incessant clam-or has dazed and hypnotized many of our girls into belief that they must not stay under the parental roof but *must* go out into the world like their brothers, to seek their fortunes. The epidemic delusion that home is no place for a girl . . . . a delusion as dangerous to the soul as the plague is to the body, seems to be gaining ground daily.

Not long ago a girl, whose father, though not sick, is quite able and willing to take care of her to help with the housework, informed me that her friends were constantly telling her she ought to be ashamed to put a burden on her Father any longer. She had about made up her mind to become a shop girl when I gave her a piece of my mind on the subject and induced her to stay at home.

An incalculable amount of harm is done by this foolish and criminal warfare on home life. Instead of being encouraged in the tendency to leave the refining atmosphere of the home, girls should be taught that, under the stress of poverty, it is selfish as well as suicidal on their part to go out and work. Selfish because they take away that which poor women and men absolutely need for their daily bread; suicidal because by offering themselves so cheaply to employees they either drive out the men or, by lowering their wages from the family standard, make it impossible for them to marry, wherefore there are some girls who had hoped, by their going out to work to increase their marriage chances, are left to die as old maids, or "new women," as they now prefer to call themselves.

There are studies which show that the chances of a girl who stays at home of retaining her virtue are many times greater than if she goes into the work force.

Ida Harper wrote the same year: "There are some very rich men so niggardly in their allowance to the members of their family that no self respecting girl, any more than a self respecting boy, will remain a dependent on their grudging bounty an hour longer than is positively necessary."

One hundred years ago there was a general consensus among American men that the role of women was to marry and spend their lives cooking, keeping the house in a clean and neat condition, have a yard and garden. Except for poor women, who had to do public work in order to eat, women were not supposed to work outside the home. There appears at that time no debate about a woman's right to vote. I always wondered what Martha Washington said when her husband, George, came home and told her that the Constitution of the United States had been approved to secure the blessings of liberty to everyone. If Martha had asked George what this constitution said about women, he would have to say, "We didn't say anything about women except we did say that for the purpose of determining the number of Representatives each state will have would be based on population and each "free person" would count as a person and I think we thought that women would be counted as a free person. "You should be pleased with this because Indians are not counted at all and Negroes only count as three-fifths of a person." To which Martha might have answered, "Many thanks."

A constitutional amendment stating that the right to vote could not be denied on account of sex, was adopted by a vote of Congress on August 20, 1920, and subsequently ratified by three-fourths of the State Legislature and became a part of our Constitution. The North Carolina Legislature, with its usual speed and dispatch continued to study this amendment, and ratified it on May 6, 1971, some 50 years after the amendment had become effective.

Along this line, at the height of the "women's lib" movement, in 1972 an equal rights amendment to the constitution was passed by Congress. To become a part of the Constitution required ratification by 3/4 of the State Legislatures and by 1975 thirty-four states had ratified the amendment, only one short of the required number. The North Carolina Legislature defeated the proposal by one vote. The amendment read, "Equality of rights under the law shall not be denied or abridged by the United States or by a State on account of sex." Section 2 provided, "Congress shall have the power to enforce, by appropriate legislation the provisions of this article." This provision would have taken away the rights of States to legislate in the area.

As the amendment came close to ratification its implications caused serous alarm, not only of men but also by some women, because of undesirable side effects, and the proposal died in March, 1979 which was the time limited by law for an amendment to the Constitution and no serious effort has been made to revive it.

As Trudy Camping said: "State action and court decisions can define rights of women. Working hour limitations, rest periods, disability leave, and weight-lifting regulations could all be handled by state legislatures, and in this manner the laws would be tempered with rationality, not included in a one-sentence (constitutional) cure all." Whether by law or not, women have proved, not only their equality, but probably their superiority. Americans are willing to fight for their country, but will not vote for those who run the country. They think that their vote won't count anyway. There is some truth in this, but there have been instances in history where one vote mattered.

By one vote, the House of Hanover won the English throne in 1701.

By one vote, France was changed from a monarchy to a republic in 1875.

By one vote, Oliver Cromwell won control of England in 1645.

By one vote, Charles I of England was executed in 1649, and they did not let him vote.

By one vote, Washington, Oregon and Idaho became part of the United States.

By one vote, Texas was admitted to the Union in 1845.

And by one vote, the German Nazi party elected as its leader in 1923 a man named Adolph Hitler.

And by one vote, the N.C. Legislature kept an amendment to the Federal Constitution from being adopted.

Wake up, America . . . your vote counts!

Much Ado About Nothing

Court was in session and an elderly woman, an obviously reluctant witness to a fight, was called to the stand to give her eyewitness account of a fracas that occurred at a Saturday night party. Her testimony: "Fact is, Judge, it actually didn't amount to nothing. First thing I know Hal Kettleson called Bill Alexander a liar and Bill knock him down with an axe handle. One of Hal's friends got kinda riled and sliced a piece of ear outa Ol' Bill. Then Howard Tweeger, who was a friend of Bill's, hit Hal over the head with a chair, then a couple of other fellows began to cut up a little here and there. Well, Judge, that naturally caused a little excitement and they commenced fighting."

REDISTRICTING

Gerrymandering

gerrymander *n. US Politics.* the dividing of a state, county, etc. into election districts so as to give one political party a majority in many districts while concentrating the voting strength of the other party into as few districts as possible.

Most citizens don't pay much attention to redistricting, I suspect because it can become so complex it discourages interest. But it is not boring, and it deserves more attention than it receives. The redistricting of legislative and congressional districts is one of the most difficult and controversial tasks of the General Assembly. It is a fascinating and fundamental part of constitutional law, government and politics in the United States.

Although ideally it shouldn't, almost all redistricting involves to some extent what we call gerrymandering. The word "gerrymander" was created in the early 1800s in the state of Massachusetts. The last name of the governor at the time was Gerry and he was involved in the creation of a voting district the shape of which resembled a salamander, which is a small lizard-like amphibian. According to John Fiske, the word came about when Governor Gerry, who was a Republican (corresponding to a Democrat in modern nomenclature), and the legislature redistricted Essex County in such a way that the towns forming the single district gave it a dragon-like contour. This was outlined upon a map of Massachusetts that Benjamin Russell, an ardent Federalist (modern Republican) and editor of *The Sentinel,* hung over the desk in his office.

The celebrated painter Gilbert Stuart came into the office one day, observed the unusual figure formed by the district, took a pencil and added a head, wings and claws. He exclaimed, "That will do for a salamander."

"Better say a gerrymander," growled the editor, and the outlandish name was born, and soon came into general use.

From then until now, the term has often been an integral part of redistricting, that is "to divide a geographical area into voting districts so as to give unfair advantage to one party in the election."

One Man, One Vote

Federal and state courts have handed down decisions, rules and regulations by the dozen. The phrase "one man, one vote" has been coined. In summary, the courts have held that every vote is to be equal with every other vote.

The most blatant example of an exception to this rule is the United States Senate, and someday the Supreme Court of the United States may rule that the United State Constitution itself is unconstitutional.

When our country was formed in the late 1700s, each of the thirteen colonies considered itself to be a sovereign state, and before they would agree to a national constitution each state wanted the same number of U.S. senators as every other sovereign state. At that time, there was not a great difference in the population of the thirteen states, and it was agreed that every state would have two senators. With fifty states today, we have one hundred senators. California, with a population right at 40 million people, and Wyoming, right at 500,000 people, each has two senators. California and Texas (20,800,000 people) have approximately a combined population of the

26 least populated states. These 26 least populated states have fifty-two senators, enough to block any legislation from being enacted by the Congress of the United States.

The Constitution of the United States, when first adopted, and now, provides that there shall be a House of Representatives. Each state was to have at least one representative. While no specific number of members was set forth, it was to be no more than one for every 30,000 people. The original House of Representatives had a total of sixty-five members. Virginia had ten, and Massachusetts and Pennsylvania each had eight. North and South Carolina each had five.

The Constitution also provided that every ten years a federal census would be taken and the states would get their proportionate share of the representatives. As a result of the 2000 census North Carolina received an extra congressman. Utah says that it should have had the extra congressman because the census did not count the Mormon missionaries serving outside their state. The Utah claim was denied in the courts. Today California has 52 representatives out of a total of 435.

The North Carolina constitution provides that our House of Representatives shall have one hundred and twenty members, and that every one of the one hundred counties shall have one representative. This leaves twenty representatives to be divided among the more populous counties. It also provides that the State Senate shall have fifty senators, who shall be elected from senatorial districts having an equal number of people with all other districts.

Then along came political parties, Republicans and Democrats, whose basic philosophies can be simply defined as whatever the other party is for, we are against. As for redistricting, both parties will move heaven and earth to create districts to assure that their party's candidates are going to win. They get a chance to do that every ten years throughout the United States, when the federal census is completed and every elective district must be changed based upon the current population.

Our method of electing our President and Vice President is fatally flawed insofar as equal representation is concerned. The electors in each state consist of the same number as the state has representatives in Congress. This is based upon population—so far, so good—but in addition, each state gets 2 electors based upon the number of Senators the state has, and each state has 2 Senators regardless of population.

Redistricting in North Carolina

For many years, the legislature redrew the congressional districts every ten years without great problems because North Carolina was growing in population, and we generally got an additional representative every ten years. More importantly, it didn't affect the district of any state legislator.

In 1941, the legislature redistricted as required. In 1951, it did not. In 1961, it did not. When I first went to the legislature in 1955, I asked an old timer why the legislature didn't do what we were obligated to do under our oath and under our constitution. His answer: "It was the obligation of the 1951 legislature and since they failed to do it, I guess we will have to wait until 1961." Nothing was done in 1961, but in 1963 Governor Terry Sanford called a special session for the purpose of redistricting the Senate.

As I remember, Sanford did not propose that the House be redistricted because there were 120 representatives and the constitutional requirement that every county would have a representative took care of 100 members, and the other twenty were pretty much taken care of between Mecklenburg, Guilford, Forsyth and Wake counties. It was not exact, but they thought it was close enough.

Sanford's 1963 special session was a total disaster. The Senate was redistricted and looked after all incumbents, but did not comply with the "one man, one vote" requirement. But that was not all the legislature did in that session. It adopted a constitutional amendment, to be submitted to a vote of the people, increasing the Senate membership from 50 to 70, and reducing the House membership from 120 to 100. (Our constitution required that every county have one representative. Thus Mecklenburg County, the most populous county, under the amendment would have one, and Perquimans County, among the least populous counties, would also have one.

To amend the constitution requires a vote of the people, and in this case, the people soundly defeated the proposed amendment. The *House Journal* showed that I voted for it. I feel sure that was a typographical mistake.

In 1965, the bomb fell. A federal court ordered the North Carolina General Assembly to redistrict. There was no escape from the order, and it meant much more than redistricting the extra twenty representatives. It meant redistricting 120 seats so that all districts would be of equal population. It meant totally redistricting the Congressional seats, the Senate seats and the House seats.

I was Speaker of the House of Representatives, Bob Scott was lieutenant governor and Dan Moore was governor. How difficult was the task for the legislature? So difficult that for twenty-five years it had not complied with the constitutional requirement. But now there was no choice.

In 1965, redistricting was not a Democrat-Republican fight, but an in-house fight among Democrats. The goal was to do nothing that would jeopardize the office of any incumbent. The congressional districts had been redistricted every ten years because of a federal mandate. The action there was more for political than population purposes. Safe districts were sought for our congressional Democrats, and the ancient process of gerrymandering was used to keep too many Republicans from congregating in any one congressional district.

Recognizing the difficulties facing the general assembly, Governor Moore, Lieutenant Governor Scott and I, as House

Speaker, met and agreed on a common strategy in seeking some consensus on redistricting. Scott would work with the Senate, I would work with the House and Moore would do the same with the congressional delegation. Little did we realize at the time that the governor had the most difficult assignment. But after several weeks, he called us to his office and said, "There's nothing I can do with that crowd. Someone else will have to get involved." As I remember it, we contacted the Democratic members of Congress and told them they had to give us a plan and they did.

Digressing for a moment . . . In North Carolina there were few problems with congressional districts. The reason being that North Carolina continued to grow in population, never losing a congressional district . . . often gaining one. This was the case in 1961. If you retained the same number, then you continued the status quo and that was fine. If you gained one, you would shuffle the counties around a little and make way for an additional member.

Here's what happened. We had one Republican congressman, Charles Jonas, from Lincolnton. The Democrats had launched mighty attacks to unseat him without success. Terry Sanford was governor and known as a liberal. My former law partner, Paul Kitchin, was in Congress and was known as a conservative. If nothing else, this proves that there are liberals and conservatives in the Democratic Party. Terry and Paul would each have liked to see the other out of office.

John Kennedy was a bright and capable young legislator from Charlotte, which was also a part of the Jonas district. Terry wanted to help him get elected. I wanted to look after Paul. As a result, the legislature created a new district that ran from Lincoln County, on the west and the home of Congressman Jonas, to Lee County on the east. It included Anson, which was Paul's home. It was pretty well agreed that there were enough Democrats in the new district to elect a Democrat.

The outcome: Kitchin beat Kennedy in the primary and Jonas beat Kitchin in the general election. It was the first indication that

Democrats would vote for Republicans . . . and on a large scale. Old Charlie was too tough for us . . .

It reminds me of the story of two men standing on the edge of a field watching a dog chase a rabbit. When thirty minutes passed and the dog had not caught the rabbit, one man observed, "I don't understand why that big dog can't catch that little rabbit." The other man replied, "There's a great deal of difference. The dog is running for the fun of it and that rabbit is running for his life." That might help to explain why congressmen are so protective of their own districts.

Back to the special session . . .

I recall that a county or combination of counties needed 45,000 people to have a legislator. That was the magic number under the "one man, one vote" rule. During one of the debates on this issue, Paul (Chalky) Wallace of Montgomery County, who rarely spoke, took the floor and said, "If you put Montgomery County with Randolph County, you will never see old Chalky again!" A tall, lanky Democrat, veteran of many sessions, Chalky was loved and respected by all members of the House. Montgomery County had only 20,000 people. Since it had less than the required 45,000, Montgomery had to be combined with one or more counties. A glance at the state map quickly revealed Chalky's problem. Stanly County to the west, Moore to the east and Richmond to the south each had about 45,000 people, so they were set. To the north was Randolph County, a Republican stronghold, with about 65,000 people. If you added the population of Montgomery and Randolph together, it was just right for two members of the House. And Chalky was correct when he added that if the counties were combined, "you will have two Republicans down here."

Representative Bill Land from Richmond County, in response to Chalky's plea, rose and made a fiery speech in defense of Montgomery County, concluding with these words, "This is a matter of principle. I'll stay here till Christmas before I vote to put old Chalky with Randolph County!"

So the House of Representatives, in its infinite wisdom, came up with an abortive scheme to link Montgomery with Hoke and Moore counties, and sent the bill to the Senate where Montgomery was promptly (and properly) put with Randolph.

To resolve the differences between the House and Senate bills, a conference committee was appointed. As Speaker of the House, I appointed three members and the president of the Senate appointed three members. Later I was walking down a corridor in the legislative building and happened to see Bill Land, who was not a member of the committee but had been called in to help resolve the differences, come out of the room in which the conference committee was meeting. I asked Bill how it was going in there.

"To hell with old Chalky!" Land replied, angrily. "He's done got my county involved in this mess." It was an entirely different situation when Land's county was being considered in a rescue effort for Montgomery, and he promptly abandoned old Chalky. Legislative love only goes so far.

Rep. Leland Brinson of Pamlico County, who also rarely spoke on the House floor, spoke out in opposition to a provision of a redistricting bill that would have combined his county with Hyde County, located north across the Pamlico Sound. Brinson, who had spent much of his life in the U.S. Navy, said that his travels had taken him to many parts if the world—Europe, Asia, Australia and South America. "But," he added, "never in my life have I been in Hyde County and now they are proposing that I represent it!"

The old motto on redistricting was: "Don't rock the boat, because someone might fall off, and it might be me."

The new motto was: "The boat's sinking and I hope I can find a life preserver."

Honorable Redistricting:
The East-West Tradition

There was an old saying that "good government is a habit in North Carolina." FDR said, "North Carolina is the most progressive state in the South." Both statements I believe were true. Some written and some unwritten laws contributed to those accolades.

We did not believe the governor should serve more than one four-year term. In addition to that, we believed that if the current governor came from eastern North Carolina, then a governor should succeed him from western North Carolina. For a long, long time we adhered to this principle.

The lieutenant governor, who served for four years, also would rotate between east and west. The Speaker of the House served for only two years, one legislative session, and would be succeeded by a Speaker from the other section of the state.

Governor Jim Hunt came up with the proposal that the constitution be amended to delete the one-term provision for both the governor and lieutenant governor. He campaigned vigorously for its passage and the legislature and the people approved it. If Governor Hunt had said that it would not apply to himself, I would have felt a little better about his sincerity that it would be good for state government. But he didn't, and he ran and was elected for a second term. In doing so, he broke two long-term traditions: the one-term governor tradition and the east-west tradition.

While the one-term provision did not apply to United States senators, the east-west tradition did. One senator always came from the east and one from the west. North Carolina is a very long state, horizontally speaking. The theory of the east-west tradition was that people should live within a reasonable distance of where their senator or governor lived and, more importantly, the needs of the people in the west were somewhat different from those in the east. Alternating between the eastern and western parts of the state also would discourage dynasties.

What happened in the last twenty-five years? Our present governor (Mike Easley) is from the coastal county of Brunswick, succeeding Jim Hunt, also from the east, and the tradition was broken for the first time in the century. Until Jesse Helms retired, both United States Senators were from Raleigh, always regarded as eastern North Carolina. The present lieutenant governor is from the east and can run for reelection. Eastern North Carolinians know how to politic and elect their candidates.

The Speakers of the House have repeatedly broken the tradition of serving only one term, and now can stay as long as they can get reelected.

President William Harrison, in his inaugural address, made a scathing indictment of succession in public office. He said it was a defect in our U.S. Constitution, with which Thomas Jefferson agreed, to allow the president to succeed himself, and he ended his remarks by renewing his pledge that under no circumstances would he consent to serve another term.

"Republicans can commit no greater error than to allow succession which is calculated to create the love of power through the long continuance in an office of high trust," Harrison said. "Nothing can be more corrupting, more destructive of the noble feelings of a patriot. It takes possession of the mind like the love of gold. It becomes insatiable. He should hold office for so short a time that he will not forget that he is an accountable agent, not the principal, the servant, not the master."

The Dark Side of Redistricting

There are two truisms in American politics:

1. People who run for public office want to win and, once they have won, they want to stay in office for life.

2. The most honorable of men will steal an election if they can. This is on the theory that they are doing the Lord's work, and anything is permissible in carrying out this noble work.

In our country, about fifty percent of the eligible voters exercise their right to vote. In one mayor's election in Charlotte, six percent voted. In a statewide gubernatorial race in Kentucky, six percent voted. Three percent voted in a statewide runoff in North Carolina for a judicial seat. In the 1996 presidential election, less than fifty percent voted, the lowest percentage in seventy years, and the 2000 vote for president was not much better. That year a higher percentage watched the Super Bowl.

Eighteen-year-olds wanted the right to vote on the theory that if they were old enough to fight for their country they were old enough to vote. They got the right and in the 1988 congressional elections a little over eight percent of them actually voted.

Stephen Hill published a book entitled *Fixing Elections: The Failure of America's Winner Take All Politics*, in 2002, which should be read by every student studying political science. He wrote:

> We have two major political parties and one of them has the majority of members in every state legislature. The importance of this lies in the fact that every ten years after the federal census it is the legislatures that redraw the district lines to comply with the population requirements and it is comparable to putting the fox in the hen house because those lines (gerrymandering) are drawn to insure the election of candidates of the majority party.
>
> What has been the result is millions of Americans are disfranchised because their candidates have no chance of winning. In addition, thousands of capable people don't run for office for the same reason.

In Charlotte a defeated Democratic candidate, in a district where Republicans outnumbered Democrats by a two to one margin, was quoted as saying, "Unless you have some miracle way of changing people's minds, there's just no point in voting or running for office."

The situation is true throughout the country and prompted Stephen Hill to write, a week before the elections: "On November 5, Americans will elect a national legislature, and we can safely make two troubling predictions about Election Day. First, barely a third of adults will participate . . . the lowest national turnout in the world among longtime democracies. Secondly, more than ninety-five percent of incumbents will cruise to victory, usually by large margins. This year we predict 332 victories for 435 seats. We make this prediction so confidently because of a simple fact . . . most districts tilt clearly toward one major party. The Fix is on.

"In redistricting, incumbents and party leaders, along with their computer consultants, have the Godlike power to draw their own district lines so as to decide in advance which party will win the next election." (*Fixing Elections: The Failure of America's Winner Take All Politics,* 2002)

The North Carolina legislature, dominated by Democrats, passed a redistricting bill that strongly favored Democrats, and the Republicans took it to Republican judges, who made changes favorable to the Republicans. It must have been somewhat fair because we ended up with 61 Republicans and 59 Democrats in our House of Representatives.

It is also important who controls the legislature in the first session after the census, because it will be the law, not just for the next election, but also for ten years and until the next census.

Interesting facts: there are 3,111 counties in the United States. In the last presidential election, George Bush carried 2,434 counties and Al Gore 677, yet Gore got the majority of the total vote.

John Adams, a conservative and no Jefferson radical, wrote that our Congress "should be in miniature an exact portrait of the people at large." If today you went in the gallery of our "People's House" in Washington, you will see our elected representatives are 86 percent white and 87 percent male. If you go over to the U.S. Senate, you will see higher percentages than this, and most of our senators are very wealthy. (Even the Roman Senate reserved twenty percent of its seats for poor members so their voices could be heard.)

EDUCATION

How to Get Into the University

Sometime around 1980 I served a term on the General Alumni Board of the University of North Carolina at Chapel Hill. It was a most enjoyable and instructive experience. I enjoyed being with my fellow board members, all of whom had a deep love for the university. We would meet on a Saturday morning at the Morehead Planetarium, then have lunch there, and at the fall meeting we would then go to the football game at Kenan Stadium.

The first major issue we were asked to resolve was: What is the true Carolina blue? A dozen or so large cards were prepared in different shades of blue. We made an extensive effort to find some historical evidence that might be of help. The purpose was to identify the exact color and copyright it and call it "true blue."

Next in importance was the issue of freshman admittance to the university. Our board took the position that an applicant for admission whose mother or father had attended the university should receive at least some degree of preference. To lobby for this position, we invited Richard Cashwell, the dean of undergraduate admissions, to talk with us at our fall meeting, and he graciously accepted. When we told him what we were advocating, he responded along these lines: "This is the biggest fool proposal I ever heard of. This is a state university, and if we ever accepted a less qualified applicant simply because his mother or father had been students here, the next morning the more qualified student and his mama and papa and their lawyer would be in our office threatening to sue."

Mr. Cashwell also explained that because there were many more applicants than the university could admit, and because it isn't possible to interview every applicant, the university had to base its decisions on class standing and SAT scores.

"Very rarely," he said, "we make exceptions for unusually talented applicants, such as a mathematical genius or an outstanding musician. As a matter of fact, you will see a good number of those exceptions playing at the football game this afternoon."

I think it's too bad that leadership cannot be included as a factor in the admissions formula.

Sports: Amateur, Professional, and Collegiate

At one time in America we had just two categories of athletes: amateur and professional. Today we have a third category called college athletes, who are not purely amateur and not fully professional.

I suspect many college and university administrators are uncomfortable with the emphasis on athletics and are troubled by the influence of television in intercollegiate sports, but at the same time they probably welcome the television money. Many of them are probably embarrassed if their football teams lose too many games, but they are probably also embarrassed, in a different way, if their teams win too many games.

Peahead Walker, the legendary Wake Forest football coach, was known for recruiting players from up North whose parents were coal miners or steelworkers. He would invite prospects to visit and meet them at the train station in Raleigh (the Wake Forest campus in those days was located just north of Raleigh, not in Winston-Salem). But instead of taking them there, he would take them to Durham and show them the Duke University campus. After recruits had signed up and come to school, some of them would ask the coach, "Where are all those pretty buildings you showed us?" Peahead would answer, "You don't get to go there until your senior year."

Peahead recalled when Wake Forest was playing Tennessee at Knoxville and he was trying to motivate his team before the game. He said to a big tackle, "Kriskowski, I want you to go out there and get ferocious today." The player said, "I will, coach. What's his number?"

Another coaching legend was Bones McKinney, a fine man who was also a preacher at times. When Bones was basketball coach at Wake Forest, the Deacons were playing N.C. State in the old gym in Raleigh, where fans would walk right in front of the coach and the players. Bones couldn't see what was happening on the court, and he finally grabbed a referee and asked him what the score was. The referee said, "We're ahead by three."

Once Bones had a player who had flunked a test and was ineligible to play in the next game. Bones went to the president of Wake Forest, explained how important the upcoming game was and begged him to show some leniency. The president said, "I'll ask him one question, and if he can answer it, I will let him play." Bones brought the player into the president's office, and the president asked him, "What is the capital of North Carolina?" The young man thought for a moment and then said, "Cary." Before the president could say anything, Bones said, "That's fine. Cary is only fifteen miles from Raleigh, so I'm sure Dr. Poteat will give you an 85, which is passing."

Consolidation and Competition

Today, North Carolina has a university system with 16 campuses. It all began with what was the first state university in the nation, established at Chapel Hill in 1795.

There are differences between a college and a university. The word "college" has many meanings, but for my purpose here I define it as an institution of higher education that does not offer graduate degrees. After the University at Chapel Hill opened its doors, the state established a number of colleges, most of them for the purpose of educating teachers for the public schools, including Western Carolina Teachers College and East Carolina Teachers College. Five of the colleges were for black students only. One, at Pembroke, was for Indians.

By 1930, three of the state's institutions could qualify as universities because they were offering doctorate degrees: the University at Chapel Hill, N.C. State College at Raleigh, and Woman's College at Greensboro. For administrative purposes, the legislature combined the three into the Consolidated University of North Carolina. One important reason for consolidation was to avoid duplication in graduate degree programs, which were expensive.

The central administrative office of the Consolidated University was placed in Chapel Hill, which did not suit the State College people at all. State people and Carolina people have never had much love for each other. The two schools competed for money in the legislature, competed for national prestige in academic circles, competed for the state's top athletes, and most of all competed on the football field and the basketball court. When I was a student at Chapel Hill and the State team was coming over for a football game, Carolina students would put banners over the streets: "Culture vs. Agriculture."

Consolidation did not diminish the competition.

East Carolina wanted to be called a university. It was more prestigious. It had the political muscle to make the change to East Carolina University. This opened the gates and the legislature changed the name of them all from college to university, except State College. They wanted to keep their name to be damn sure that they had no connection with Chapel Hill.

Three in One

When the legislature was writing the law to restructure higher education in North Carolina, putting all the state's campuses under one Board of Governors, one issue was how to ensure representation on the new board for all citizens, of every race, gender and political affiliation.

The first draft provided that there should be at least "one Black, one woman and one Republican." I was lieutenant governor at the time, and a black friend came to my office and said that provision needed to be rewritten.

"The way it reads now," he said, "you all could appoint Judge Alexander and kill three birds with one stone." Judge Alexander, from Guilford County, was black, a woman and a Republican.

The Importance of Student Aid

Jack Coggin was a successful businessman and a state senator who was orphaned as a child. When he finished high school in the orphanage, he applied and was admitted to the University at Chapel Hill. When he arrived at the campus, the first person he went to see was Ed Lanier, the student aid director, who later became state insurance commissioner.

Jack told Mr. Lanier that he had arrived at Chapel Hill with 30 dollars and had put 20 dollars down for admission and 10 dollars for a dormitory room.

Ed said, "Jack, I'm very impressed with you and I am going to see what I can do for you."

Jack said, "Thank you, Mr. Ed, but I want you to remember that while you are thinking about what you can do for me, I'm not eating."

Students who have to work their way through college get a lot better education than those who major in fraternities, football and basketball.

The Limitations of Politics

While I was serving on the board of trustees at UNC-Greensboro, I made a suggestion that received less support than any proposal I ever made in the political field.

A group of businessmen in Greensboro wanted UNC-G to have an outstanding men's basketball team that could compete with those at UNC-Chapel Hill and N.C. State. They offered to raise $250,000 to help UNC-G establish a big-time basketball program. The athletic director at UNC-G was a nice lady who had a Ph.D. from Ohio State University, and I suspect she might have been Woody Hayes' sister. When the business group made the offer, she said, "That's just fine if they want to give us $250,000. We certainly would appreciate it, but I can tell you this: the women's team is going to get half of it."

That killed the idea, because the business group wasn't interested in women's basketball, so I made a suggestion. "It seems to me that you have two large state universities within two miles of each other in the same city. Why don't you merge the two institutions, save a bunch of money by removing duplication of programs, administrators, etc., and you will have your basketball team immediately."

I was referring to N.C. A&T, also in Greensboro, a predominantly black college that had a men's basketball program. Even though I was only half serious, I thought there was merit to the idea, but no one else agreed. N.C. A&T expressed its opposition in a resolution and UNC-G was vigorously opposed.

Later, Bill Friday, president of the university system, told me, "You know, I've been giving thought to that same proposition for a long time, but there are just some things in the political world you can do, and some things you cannot do."

I still think it ought to be done.

Year-Round Schools

When I was a candidate for governor in 1972 I gave a detailed outline of plans for public education in the future. It included a proposal for staggered year-round school attendance. I would have done better to keep that part quiet until after the election. My advisors told me to stop talking about it. They said schoolchildren all over the state were organizing to protest that "Pat Taylor is going to make us go to school in the summer." I replied, "School children can't vote." They said, "Well, their parents damn well can!"

I thought it was a good idea then and I still do. There were no such programs in 1972, but twenty years later there were 16 districts in the state with year-round school programs. Editorials have begun to praise the idea.

The school calendar is something of an anachronism. It was created to meet the needs of a rural society in which children needed to be at home in the summer months to help with work on the family farm. It does not meet any such need today. Many families might prefer that their children have a longer midwinter break. Year-round school would not mean that any child would be in class twelve months of the year. It would simply mean more choices for families, more flexibility for schools and better use of facilities.

One reason we have had difficulty getting teacher pay to the level where it ought to be is that teachers traditionally only taught for nine months each year and were only paid for nine months. Today it's more like ten months, but the principle still applies. They should be employed for twelve months and paid for twelve months, with liberal vacations and preparation time outside the classroom. Most college professors are employed for twelve months of the year.

School enrollments are increasing by leaps and bounds in some parts of North Carolina, requiring counties to build more classrooms. There is something flawed with a system that has to have new buildings, but all of its buildings are unoccupied and unused for one-quarter of each year.

A twelve-month school year also would create more opportunities for remedial programs, which I understand is a growing need.

Most important, perhaps, is that educators have said children learn more efficiently on a calendar that doesn't break for three months every year.

Logic

A teacher was trying to explain logic to her sixth-grade class.

She said, "The United States is bounded on the north by Canada, on the east by the Atlantic Ocean, on the south by Mexico, and on the west by the Pacific Ocean. How old am I?"

A little boy raised his hand and said, "44."

The teacher said, "That's right, Johnny. Now tell the class how you used logic to come up with the answer."

Johnny said, "Well, I've got a brother at home. He's half crazy, and he's 22."

Young People in Revolt - 1970

Dedicated to those who don't remember how serious the rebellion of young people was in the 1960s and '70s.

Governor Scott was out of the country. He directed his office to advise me, as Lieutenant Governor, of any threatened violence. A civil intelligence bulletin from the State Bureau of Investigation contained:

African weekend activities, A&T:
5.16.70 Meeting and speech by "Brother" Mainza Shona, for the Republic of Zambia. The speech will be followed by a speech from Howard Fuller. After this there will be a special tribute to Malcolm X.

Fayetteville: After checking all reliable sources such as military intelligence it would appear that an estimated 5,000 students will take part in a peace rally to be held on May 16, 1970. Several buses of students are expected to leave the campuses of NCSU, UNCCH and Duke.

Oxford: Last night, as a result of the curfew, 10 weapons were seized at various checkpoints in Oxford. Six fire bombs were thrown. Ben

Chavis spoke and then introduced Arch Foster, who is connected with the Black Panthers. After the speeches they lined up two abreast and marched.

Cullowee: It is reported that approximately 8,000 to 10,000 hippy-type students are expected at Western Carolina University for the "Rock Music Festival," which will climax tomorrow and the rest of the weekend.

What is a Dangerous Weapon?

In the 1960's the ophthalmologists of North Carolina (eye doctors) had a bill introduced in the legislature that would declare an air rifle (B.B. gun) to be a dangerous weapon and thereby be subject to an existing law which made it unlawful for a parent to permit a child under 12 years of age to possess, or use, a dangerous firearm unless the child was under the supervision of a parent. The reason for the proposed bill arose out of the fact that some judge had ruled that an "air rifle" was not a dangerous weapon. The ophthalmologists showed the members of the committee that were considering the bill charts which showed that beginning on Christmas Day, and for two weeks thereafter, the number of children injured by air rifles skyrocketed. We were all ready to approve the bill. Then along came the National Rifle Association and vigorously opposed it on the grounds that it was depriving citizens of the right to bear arms. It was a classic example of the political power of the NRA, and the legislature would not approve the bill. Those of us who supported it had amended it so that the law would only apply to the counties we represented. So long as it did not apply to their county, the other legislators voted for it. The result was that in 13 counties (which includes Anson County) an air rifle is a dangerous weapon and in 87 counties it is not.

One Language

Wars are going on all over the world. We may be further from peace than we have ever been. In a world of terrorism, the size of your army is not that meaningful. Common sense would tell us that there is a lack of communication between conflicting interests. A meaningful step toward finding a solution might be to get all nations of the world to agree to one language that would be taught in every country. Every nation could keep its native language, but this plan would insure that everyone in the world could not only speak the same language, but also read anything written in the international language. If a Paris cab driver can speak French, German and English, surely everyone can learn two languages.

Free Education

Our constitution provides: "The people of the State have a right to the privilege of education and it is the duty of the State to guard and maintain that right.

"The benefits of the University of North Carolina, and other public institutions of higher education, as far as practicable be extended to the people of the State free of expense."

I can only assume that "as far as practicable" means it is not practicable if the legislature doesn't provide the money. It would be interesting to see what the Supreme Court would say about it.

Practical Education

A sixteen-year-old farm boy was doing poor academically in school and was asked by the principal as to what was causing his poor performance. He wrote in part: "I don't know exactly why I don't make good grades. Like when the teacher asked me to write a paper as to how to set out tobacco, I did real well on that. But last week she asked us to write a paper on 'what a daffodil thinks of spring.' I just couldn't get started on that."

Latin

The state motto of North Carolina is "Esse Quam Videri," which in Latin means, "To Be Rather Than to Seem." As I listen to candidates for public office on television, I often think the motto should be "Videri Esse Quam." Whatever happened to Latin? When I was in school Latin was supposed to be as important as arithmetic. A country preacher announced one Sunday morning that his sermon was to be on the "Status Quo," and added, "In case some of you don't know what that means, it am Latin for the mess we is in."

The News and Observer
and the Environment

The News and Observer has been discussed and cussed about politics for a hundred years. During legislative days in my time, legislators would stay up until the *News and Observer* came out so they could read "Under the Dome." It had a substantial affect on the politics of North Carolina, particularly eastern North Carolina.

The old *News and Observer* used to be right controversial in eastern North Carolina basically arising out of its political positions. I had a friend from Rocky Mount who was an airplane pilot and a crop duster. One day he had just flown over a cotton field when he felt a pain in his right foot. When he landed, he took off his shoes and discovered he had been shot, which was confirmed by finding a hole in the bottom of the plane. He called the Sheriff and they went out to a house at the south end of the field. The Sheriff knocked on the door and a somewhat unsober man came to the door. The Sheriff said, "This gentleman was dusting the field next to your house this morning and he said he got shot. Do you know anything about it?" "I sure do," was the reply. "I shot the son of a bitch. He done ruined my garden with all that poison and I shot him." The farmer was charged with assault with a deadly weapon.

My friend, I think his name was Roddy, told me, "And I'll be damned if the *News and Observer* didn't write an editorial in favor of the fellow that shot me."

Short-Term Solutions

President Nixon told a story intended to illustrate that short-term solutions to a problem are not always in the best interest of those involved. Nixon was a naval officer in WWII. His duty was to keep the base and its property in good working order. The Inspector General was constantly complaining that the toilet bowls had rings inside the commode. Nixon asked a seasoned and long-time first sergeant about the problem. The sergeant said he would attend to the matter, and he did to the total satisfaction of the Inspector General's office. Nixon highly praised the sergeant and asked him how he solved the problem. His reply, "Well, there's generally speaking a way to solve any problem, but the best way ain't always the quickest way. In this case I used red devil lye. It does a wonderful job on the bowl but it eats up the pipes." When Congress spends more than it takes in, it might solve some problems but it creates a problem of paying it back.

Fishing in Elizabeth City

When I was Lieutenant Governor I went to Elizabeth City for some occasion and visited a plant that made television cabinets for, I believe, RCA. The plant was located in an old dirigible hanger that was used during World War II to fly over the ocean looking for German submarines. After the war was over, the government gave the hangars to Pasquotank County for industrial development.

I was talking with the manager of the plant and asked him how he liked North Carolina. He said, "I like it fine, but I would never put another plant here." Naturally I asked him why. His answer, "I have half a work force today. I was looking out the window this morning and saw cars come to the gate, turn around and leave. I went to the gate guard to find out what was going on and discovered he was telling the employees 'the herring started running today' and they would turn around and head home. These people would rather fish than work."

Medical Expenses

Ed Rankin and I were on the noard of directors of Blue Cross Blue Shield for a number of years. As medical expenses began escalating at an alarming rate, Blue Cross found there was a wide disparity between charges of physicians for the same procedure. In an effort to prevent excessive charges, Blue Cross retained a panel of distinguished doctors and asked them to formulate a list of various medical treatments and tell what a reasonable charge would be for the different procedures. When this was completed, Blue Cross sent out notices containing a list of procedures for which reimbursement would be made and the amount to be paid for each item. Well, you would have thought World War III had started. The doctors called it everything from communism and socialism to unlawful price fixing. Only a small percentage of doctors signed agreements to cooperate with the program, which was designed to reduce the costs of medical care.

Blue Cross had a hidden weapon. It advised the doctors who would not join the program that they could charge anything they wanted to charge, however, Blue Cross would send the checks to their policyholders and not to the doctors. The doctors then realized that many of these checks would never reach the doctor's office which resulted in practically all of the doctors joining the program.

What Have You Done For Me Lately?

Americans were rather harsh on France when it failed to support us in the war on Iraq. Some advocated changing the name of French fries. They called them ingrates for not remembering what we did for France in World Wars I and II. Maybe we ought to also remember that when Cornwallis surrendered at Yorktown, thus ending the Revolutionary War, there were 9,000 American troops and 7,000 French troops. A history book says: "There can be no question that without France's armies, money and supplies the American forces could not have won." (As much as 90 percent of the American gunpowder used in the war came from France.)

How I Gave Away $100,000

When I was Lieutenant Governor I received a call from Philadelphia from a gentleman who introduced himself and said, "Governor Taylor, I would like for you to come to Philadelphia to see me." I asked about what. He said, "I can't tell you about what over the telephone but I promise that if you come you will not regret it." I said, "I feel sure you are right but I simply can't come with no more information than I have." He said, "Well, if you won't come to see me I will come to see you." I said, "That will be fine and I will be glad to see you." He asked, "Where is the nearest airport to where you live?" I said, "Charlotte," and we arranged to meet at 10:00 A.M. on the following Saturday.

I asked my lifelong friend John Stedman who was in the banking business in Charlotte to go with me, and we met the Philadelphia plane and met the gentleman. He was well-dressed and a nice looking person but didn't look like a preacher exactly. I had arranged for a room at the airport.

On this particular day Mohammed Ali was the heavyweight champion of the world, but he bad been convicted of draft evasion and sentenced to a term in the big house. To say that he was unpopular would be an understatement. He had appealed his case to the Supreme Court of the United States, after having lost in the Court of Appeals and the Las Vegas odds were 5 to 1 that his next fight would be an intramural fight between Alcatraz and Attica.

This was the proposition: "I have the rights to a fight between Ali and Frazier," the man said. Frazier was the leading contender for the title. "The New York Athletic Commission has turned down the fight, likewise Pennsylvania. I understand North Carolina either doesn't have a Boxing commission or if it does it is not much of one. If you can arrange the fight in North Carolina, I will give you $100,000 in cash and another $100,000 for your favorite charity. We are desperate to have the fight before the Supreme Court rules because we don't think the Champ will be able to get out on work release." He further said, "Mr. Taylor, if you can't arrange to have the fight on land we can have it off the coast of North Carolina and the ship can be half in international waters. I asked him why it had to be half and half. He said, "Because Mohammed is out on bond and he cannot leave the country and the fight will have to be on the half of the ship that is in coastal waters."

At the time I was planning to run for governor and I thought it might not set too well with my constituents and I turned him down. A month or so later the fight was held in Atlanta and I watched it in a movie house and the first person I saw in the ring before the fight was a fat Georgia senator in a white linen suit like Colonel Sanders wore and I knew immediately who had my $100,000.

As events unfolded, instead of being a bum I would have been a hero, particularly if I had given my $100,000 to charity.

Have You Ever Been Lost?

When I think some program is not very practical, I tell the story about a boy in eastern North Carolina who was walking down a country road when a big, black Cadillac came down the road with a New York license plate. It stopped and the driver rolled the window down and asked, "Sonny, do you know how far it is to Jonesboro?" The little boy said, "The way you're going, it's 24,997 miles, but if you turn around it's three miles back that way."

Sometimes I don't think we know exactly where we are going. A conductor on a train called to a porter working in the freight car. A mule was being shipped by train and had a tag around his neck showing its destination. "Joe, look and see where that mule is going." Joe went back to look and called back to the conductor, "Boss, that mule done et where he's going."

Sin and Politics

Gambling

When I was a child in Sunday School we were taught that gambling was a sin. This was in a Baptist church and I have forgotten what scripture was cited in support of the proposition. It might have been that you couldn't tithe if you lost all your money gambling. Or it could have been that you can't love your neighbor as yourself if you take his property for nothing. In any event, it was definitely considered very bad.

Later, I went to a Presbyterian school, McCallie, in Chattanooga, Tennessee. The way to get there from Wadesboro was to take the train to Atlanta on the Seaboard Air Line Railroad, change stations and take the C&O to Chattanooga. Before the train got to South Carolina, there were several other boys headed to McCallie, and someone suggested a poker game. The idea met with general acceptance and the game was on all the way to our destination.

At our first assembly, the headmaster, Dr. J.P. McCallie, welcomed us to the school. A large placard over the speaker's rostrum read: "The chief end of man is to glorify God and enjoy Him forever." At McCallie, religion came before education, but we got a head full of both.

Dr. McCallie taught the New Testament, and on one occasion he told his class that the sole purpose of sexual intercourse between a man and a woman was for procreation, and that he and his wife had never had intercourse except for the purpose of having children. This was very hard for 17- and 18-year-old boys to understand.

It was 1940–41 and all the missionaries were returning home from China and Japan. Dr. McCallie felt he had an obligation to invite them to speak to the student body. All the speeches were the same, and with great temerity some of the students prepared a petition to Dr. McCallie saying that they had no objection to hearing every missionary who came to Chattanooga, but they didn't think he had to invite every missionary who came to Tennessee. There were ten or more of us who prepared the petition, but when it was finished and the time for signing came, not a single one of us had the courage to sign it. But one brave boy said he would be willing to slip the petition under Dr. McCallie's office door. Dr. McCallie never mentioned it and I don't think it helped or hurt because by that time we had heard about all of the missionaries.

My senior year at McCallie, I was the class poet. There was a banquet the night before graduation and my duty was to say something about each senior. One of our classmates had a sweetheart who attended Girl's Preparatory School (GPS) in Chattanooga. The love affair between the two had gone on for an extended period of time. World War II was in full force in Europe. Hitler and his troops had overrun France and conditions were pretty bad in England. There was a national volunteer program in the United States called "Bundles for Britain" and families would prepare boxes of food and clothing that were sent to the English people.

I wrote this about the love-stricken couple:

> *Bill and Mary went a-courting.*
> *What they did they ain't admitting,*
> *But what she's knitting ain't for Britain.*

Two hours before graduation, Dr. McCallie sent for me, closed the door of his office and said, among other things, that my poem was not in keeping with the principles of McCallie School. "If it were not for it being graduation day, I would most seriously discipline you!"

All of this is background for the subject of this section: gambling. At our first school assembly, Dr. McCallie said that gambling was very wrong, a sin and that if students had gambled on their train trip to the school then he wanted anyone who had won any money to give it back to those who lost. This caused right much debating among my classmates. The losers tried to get their money back. The winners' philosophy was "winners keeping, losers weeping" and "possession is nine-tenths of the law." I don't think any money changed hands, but Dr. McCallie certainly didn't do anything for the Christian doctrine of brotherly love.

As for gambling in North Carolina, our history tells us that in the 1700s and 1800s horse racing was a popular sport. Races were usually held over a period of three days, and the roads were crowded with visitors from the country and neighboring villages. Bets ran high and there was a tremor of excitement pervading the whole community. It is what today we call the Kentucky Derby. Each day was duly concluded with a ball that was attended by the fashionable and beautiful people of the surrounding counties.

An old man, gray-haired and in tattered clothes, was at the racetrack. He approached a bookie and asked what the odds were on Old Joe in the sixth race. The bookie said, "Look, old man, you look like my father and I can see you are right much down on your luck. The odds are fifty to one on Old Joe and I can promise you he can't win."

The old man said, "I'll put $100 on Old Joe." Reluctantly, the bookie took the bet. A little while later, the old man came back. The odds had gone to seventy-five to one and he invested another $50. Finally, just before the sixth race, the old man came back. The odds were 100 to one and he wanted to bet another $50.

The bookie, shaking his head, said, "Old man, I told you that you reminded me of my father. I told you Old Joe just couldn't win. The reason I know Old Joe can't win is because I own Old Joe and I have told the jockey not to let him win."

The old man replied, "Well, you are going to see the slowest horse race in history, because I own the other three horses in the race."

As early as 1810, an attempt was made, largely by the clergy, to outlaw horse racing, but all efforts to make the sport illegal were defeated. Since betting at a race was universal in the sport, an effort was made to outlaw betting. In 1810, a bill was passed that prevented recovery of any bets made on a race. In other words, if you lost money betting on a race, the winner could not take you to court and recover. This promoted a requirement that if you bet, you put up the money in advance.

In the earliest reports by the Supreme Court of North Carolina, gambling was a frequent topic of controversy and concern. In *N.C. Reports*, the Supreme Court held (*Sharpe vs. Murphy*, p.568) that a horseracing contract had to be in writing to be enforceable (1802).

In *Haywood Reports*, 2NC502 (1797), the Court held that when two men entered into a written contract to run a mare against a horse, $1,000 would go to the winner with a penalty of $400 if either failed to run on the day set forth for the race. After the contract was made, the mare became lame and died. The court held that the defendant whose horse had died was liable for the $400 because that was a rule of racing.

In *Haywood Reports*, New Bern in 1803, the plaintiff sued to recover money that he had lost in a card game. The court held that, under the common law, money lost in a card game could not be recovered in a legal action. There was a law that provided, "Every transfer of slaves, or other personal estate to satisfy money won in a card game was void." In 1804, in a similar case (3NC297), the judge ruled, "The act should be so construed as to suppress the vice of gaming, which is the parent of every misfortune; and the best way to do this is to give no action to the plaintiff in such a case. For knowing that he will not be relieved, he will take care not to engage in gambling."

In the Supreme Court of North Carolina, in *State vs. Lumpkin* (169NC265), the court said, in part: "Like any other species of gambling, lotteries have a pernicious influence upon the character of all engaged in them. This influence may be a direct and the immediate consequence as disastrous as in some kinds of gambling which rouse the passions and stake the gamblers' whole fortune upon the throw of a dice."

The Supreme Court of the United States wrote an opinion (8Howard168): "The North Carolina Beneficial Association is an imposing title, but the law has pronounced it in its lottery features to be a cheat and a nuisance to be suppressed like other public perturbances. Of all forms of gambling, it is the most widespread and disastrous, entering about every dwelling, reaching every class, preying upon the hard earning of the poor and the ignorant and the simple."

In *Hodges vs. Pittman,* the Supreme Court of North Carolina wrote: "We feel not less disposed than the able men who have gone before us, so to expand the law is to promote the practice of private virtue, and check the growth of this most ruinous vice of gambling. It is clear that gambling is a proper subject for either complete prohibition or conditional regulation under the police power. It is also evident without need of citation that the promotion of general charitable, civic, education and public safety is a proper object of legislation."

There are other forms of gambling that are a part of North Carolina history. During the same years of horse racing there was cockfighting, which was popular and prevalent. Easter Sunday was a popular time for fights, but there were also regular fall and spring contests. On the day of a contest, all roads leading to the town where the main event was to be held were alive with carriages, horses and pedestrians. The cock pit might be at a tavern, country store or at a spacious square near the center of town. The cocks were often beautiful and well-trained fowls. Each was armed with long steel-pointed gaffs firmly attached to its spurs. Amid the lusty shouts of the crowd, the birds stepped proudly about, advancing nearer and nearer to each other until with a rush each bird attempted to drive its gaffs into the body of its opponent. Both or either might be struck dead at the first thrust, but if not they fought on with great spirit. Even after repeatedly being pierced, the birds would continue to make stabs as long as they were able to move or crawl. Large sums of money were bet on each fight.

From early on, cockfighting was looked upon as barbarous and irreligious. In 1810, Moore County stopped it as being contrary to benevolence and humanity. When a bill was introduced in the 1824 legislature to suppress the sport, it was immediately defeated. However, other laws have been enacted down through the state's history, all of which recognized the unwholesome nature of gambling or gaming.

In 1764, it was made illegal to win more than five shillings within a 24-hour period. Several laws against "excessive gain" were passed in colonial days, but the first drastic law came in 1791 when public gaming tables were forbidden and subject to a fine of $2,000. The law was reinforced in 1798 and again in 1799. In 1835, it was made an indictable offense to play at a gambling table of any variety. A year earlier, lotteries, which had been popular in the first quarter of the century as a means of raising monies for academies, churches and lodges, were forbidden at a penalty of $2,000.

There was gambling, of course, in spite of these laws. Alexander Snead of Rockingham in 1810 referred to "that violent, abominable practice of card playing which is so prevalent at our courthouses, taverns, et cetera." (*N.C. Historical Review*, 1810) Without any attempt to review the total history of gambling in North Carolina, there is no doubt that gambling has been held to be unwholesome and not in the best interest of the general welfare of our people. Suffice it to say that for the past 100 years by state law it has been illegal to gamble in North Carolina.

G.S. 14-292 reads: "Any person or organization that operates any game of chance or any person who plays or bets on any game of chance at which any money or property or other things of value is bet, whether the same be in stake or not, is guilty of a misdemeanor (crime)." A liberal reading of this makes it a crime to match coins for a drink, to bet on a golf game, baseball, football or basketball game, or to play poker.

A State Lottery?

Article I of the constitution of North Carolina sets forth a Declaration of Rights (comparable to the Bill of Rights of the federal Constitution). Section 35 is entitled "Recurrence to Fundamental Principles" and reads as follows: "A frequent recurrence of fundamental principles is absolutely necessary to preserve the blessing of liberty." This has been a part of our constitution since 1868.

What does it mean? It certainly means that there is such a thing as "fundamental principles." Is it a fundamental principle that gambling does not promote the general welfare of the people of the state? Principles are defined by my dictionary as a comprehensive and fundamental law, doctrine or assumption, or a rule or code of conduct. They are fundamental as of or relating to essential structure, function or facts of central importance. A strong case can be made that opposition to gambling is and has been a fundamental principle in the law of North Carolina.

This brings me to the question of whether or not the State of North Carolina ought to operate a lottery. Our present governor, Mike Easley, favors it. Many other states have state-run lotteries. When those who support the measure talk about their support being influenced by other states, it reminds me of my childhood. I would ask my mother if I could do something. She would say no. I would ask why, and she would reply, "Because I said so." I would say "Everybody else is doing it," and she would say, "I don't care what everybody else is doing, you are not going to do it."

Rationally, how can the state have a law that has been in effect for over 100 years—not a regulatory law but a criminal law that a person can be imprisoned for violating—and now engage in the same activity? Would it not be consistent to repeal the existing law that prohibits seven million people from gambling, and that they would violate if they even bought a lottery ticket? Do we believe that gambling was wrong in the 18th, 19th and 20th centuries, but is now right? If so, we should repeal all laws that prohibit gambling because it is now a good thing to do.

Would you like Charlotte or Raleigh patterned after Las Vegas? I saw in a recent news article that some people in Las Vegas, now known as the Gambling Capital of America, want their community to be known as "Sin City," so that it will include not just gambling but also sex.

An argument is made that the profits will go to improve education. Nobody, they say, can oppose that. The state, with so many laws regulating the use of alcohol and recognizing its threat, now is in the business of promoting alcohol. What about selling marijuana or heroin or cocaine and using the profits for education?

Alcohol and gambling are both addictive. Both used or engaged in, in moderation, may not be harmful; however, it is universally accepted that a certain percentage of people cannot use or participate in moderation. I know a prominent citizen in North Carolina who spent a week in Las Vegas and lost $100,000 more than he had. Enforcers were sent to see him and he was paying $2500 a month to the casinos. Even so, one of his friends told me he would slip back to Las Vegas on occasion and still gamble.

The only thing that ever appealed to me about a lottery was this: Most people in this country are poor and have no hope of ever being rich, but they can buy a lottery ticket and go to sleep and dream, happy and content, all night long, of winning a big lottery prize and waking up rich.

It has been said with truth that every great nation in the history of the world has finally collapsed due to becoming affluent, with the moral decadence that has followed and caused its downfall. The Roman Empire ruled the world and its citizens became rich and in the process Rome lost its moral strength and stamina that had made it great and it fell. There is an old saying, "history repeats itself." Can this be happening in America today?

I hope the General Assembly of North Carolina will not legalize a state lottery. If it does I hope the legislators will have the courage to do it themselves. Every citizen in the state has the opportunity to elect his or her representatives and senators. For them to submit this question to a referendum, a vote of the people, could be comparable to Pilate turning Jesus over to the crowd. Sometimes people need to be protected from themselves.

In gambling, for every winner there is a loser, and as a general principle the loser is the one who can least afford to lose. Gambling is the antithesis of "honest pay for an honest day's work." Instead, its motto is "something for nothing." In a lottery there are millions of losers for every winner. If a law hurts more people then it helps, it is a bad law.

THAT OLD-TIME RELIGION

A Baptist Boyhood

In the western part of North Carolina, there are mostly Baptists, Methodists and Presbyterians and a small percentage of Episcopalians, which was the Mother Church of the aristocrats down east. I heard an Episcopal bishop explain this phenomenon. He said the Baptists sent missionaries to Indian Territory when there were only trails to travel by, the Methodists waited until there were some public roads and the Episcopalians waited until there were Pullman cars on the railroads.

Bishop Frazier, an Episcopal clergyman, said that when he was ordained, he was sent to a small town in Georgia where there were only three churches, Episcopal with 40 members, Presbyterian with 60 members, and Baptist with 800 members. He hadn't been there a month before the Baptists got in a fuss and it was about to break up not only the church, but also the town. Bishop Frazier went downtown to get his mail one morning and ran into the Presbyterian minister. The bishop said, "Isn't it terrible about the Baptists?" To which the other responded, "Don't you worry about the Baptists. They're like cats. When you think they are fighting, all they're doing is multiplying."

Growing up in the Great Depression, children had to get along without many things we would like to have had, but religion was not one of those things. My mother and father were Baptists and it was understood that their children would be Baptists. There was no freedom of choice. As good Baptist children, we were expected to go to Sunday School, Sunday morning church service, BYPU (Baptist Young People's Union) on Sunday evening, and Sunday night church service. Then there was choir practice, prayer meeting on Wednesday night, and Royal Ambassadors on Friday. We said a blessing before every meal and a prayer before we went to bed. In the summer, there was Vacation Bible School. The only optional activity was a week at Ridgecrest, a Baptist retreat in the mountains.

Baptists went to church often but, like most people, didn't want to stay past the allotted time. In the 1930s, a new Baptist church was built in Wadesboro. On the railing across the balcony, the board of deacons placed a large clock that faced the pulpit, so the preacher would know when it was twelve o'clock and time for him to end his sermon. When this didn't work, there was some talk of putting an alarm on the clock.

Many parents required their children "get up their lessons" on Saturday because everyone knew it was not proper to study anything but the Bible on Sunday. Many thought that playing cards was a sin any time, but particularly on Sunday. The "picture show" owner in Wadesboro wanted to open on Sunday afternoon and there was a referendum to allow it. It was defeated.

Drinking alcohol was a big sin any time, but I knew that my parents probably drank alcohol, because I found where it was hidden. When they had company, they would shut the doors to the living room, and I was pretty sure some of them were having a drink.

One Sunday morning, our preacher devoted the whole sermon to the sin of drinking, and at the end he asked everyone in the congregation to stand and promise they would never take another drink. All the women immediately stood, and some of them were trying to pull their husbands up. Finally one husband broke ranks, and before it was over everyone was standing.

The Kentucky Baptist convention was meeting at a large dining establishment near Lexington some years ago. They were in one dining hall and a convention of Shriners was in the other dining hall. For dessert, the Baptists were having ice cream and cake. The Shriners were having watermelon soaked in bourbon whisky. Somehow the waiters got things mixed up and served the Shriners the ice cream and cake and the Baptists the watermelon. When the owner of the establishment found out, he took the headwaiter to task.

"Now look here, John, you have been with me for 40 years. You know what I expect of every person here. You have ruined me. It's awful. You know those Baptist preachers did not eat that watermelon soaked in bourbon whisky."

Old John looked up and said, "Cap'n Jim, not only did they eat it, but the last time I looked, they was stuffing the seeds in their pockets."

Here's a riddle: Why should you always take two Baptists with you when you go fishing? Answer: If you take just one, he will drink all your beer.

In North Carolina, at least until fairly recently, public attitudes and political positions regarding alcohol have been heavy with hypocrisy and sometimes inconsistent. In 1881, there was a statewide referendum on the question: "Are you for or against prohibition?" This meant, of course, prohibition of the manufacture and sale of alcoholic beverages. The vote was 48,370 for prohibition and 166,345 against. Twenty-seven years later (1908), in another referendum on the same question, the vote was 113,612 for prohibition and 69,416 against.

North Carolina is a state of Baptists. They are by far the largest denomination. A young man was sent to state prison in Raleigh and he wrote his mother a letter. "Don't worry about me," he wrote. "They are treating me good down here. You'll be glad to know that down here it is like everywhere else . . . we Baptists is in the lead."

A farmer invited his city cousin to visit. They went for a ride and the city cousin noticed at a crossroad there was a Baptist church on one side of the road and another Baptist church on the other side of the road. Why, he asked, were there two Baptist churches so close to each other? The farmer replied: "Theology. The church on the right believes Pharaoh's daughter found Moses in the bulrushes. The members of the other church say that Pharaoh's daughter said she found Moses in the bulrushes."

I guess that's why we have so many different Christian denominations. I don't believe that when you get to the Pearly Gates Saint Peter is going to ask you what church you were a member of.

Religion and Money

Money has always been a matter of right much importance in small town and country churches. It would not be a problem if all the members would tithe. To tithe is supposed to mean giving 10 percent of your income to the church. But some members who obey every other commandment and who claim to tithe devise their own formulas. A good illustration was my long-time dear friend, Gus Zollicoffer.

Gus and I were talking about this and that and the subject got around to religion. Gus acknowledged that he was a Christian and believed in the Bible and abided by the rules set forth therein. Knowing that he was somewhat careful in his expenditures, I asked him if he believed in tithing. He said he did.

"Do you tithe?" I asked.

"I sure do," he said.

"Do you mean to tell me you give 10 percent of your income to the church?"

"Well, not exactly," he said. "I am trying to raise my children in a Christian home, and I count a part of the household expenses toward my tithe."

I said, "I guess you also deduct it on your income tax."

A preacher in a country church stood up one Sunday and had a sort of spontaneous responsive reading with his congregation.

"This church has got to get up and walk," he said.

Congregation: "Walk, brother, walk."

"This church has got to get up and run."

Congregation: "Run, brother, run."

"This church has got to get up and fly."

Congregation: "Fly, brother, fly."

"It takes money to fly."

Congregation: "Walk, brother, walk."

One Sunday morning four strangers attended the service at the Baptist Church in Wadesboro. Everybody at the service knew they were a pulpit committee from some out-of-town church looking for a new preacher, and obviously considering ours.

After the service, our preacher and his wife ate Sunday dinner with the strangers at a restaurant, according to the spies our church sent to follow them. Our board of deacons held a secret meeting that afternoon and decided to send two deacons to the parsonage to face the crisis head-on. They knocked on the front door and the preacher's 12-year-old son answered.

"Jimmy, who were those foreigners in church this morning, the ones you ate dinner with?"

"They're from Asheboro," he said.

"What did they want?"

"They want Daddy to go to Asheboro and be their preacher. They offered him $1,000 a year more than he's getting paid here."

"Where is your father now?"

"He's upstairs in his study praying and asking the Lord what he should do."

"Where's your mother?"

"She's in her room packing."

When our daughter, Beth, was six years old her mother and I put her on what then was called an allowance. It was 50 cents a week to use as she wished, except that she had to put a nickel of it in the church collection plate each Sunday. One night after the first Sunday under that arrangement, her mother was putting her to bed. Beth kneeled down by the bed, closed her eyes, and said: "Now I lay me down to sleep, I pray the Lord my soul to keep. If I should die before I wake, I pray thee Lord my soul to take. God bless Mama and Daddy and Hoyt and Lockhart. And God, please let me have a puppy, and God, don't forget that we're paying you for this. Amen."

Matters of Faith

A little boy came home from Sunday School and his mother asked him what the lesson had been about. "Moses," he said.

"What about Moses?" she asked.

"The children of Israel," he said, "were held as hostages in Egypt and they wanted to escape. So one night Moses, who was the general, built a pontoon bridge across the Red Sea and was slipping the children out. Moses looked through his binoculars and saw the Egyptian tanks chasing them. He got on his walky-talky radio and called his artillery and told them to blow up the bridge when the children got across, and they did, and all the tanks fell into the ocean and the Egyptians were drowned and Moses and the children got away."

"Is that what your teacher said?" his mother asked.

"Well, not exactly. But if I'd told you what she really said, you never would have believed it."

A tourist was visiting the Great Smoky Mountains in western North Carolina. He climbed a rather tall mountain and was standing at the top looking at the magnificent view when he slipped and fell off. There was a 1,000-foot drop, and he was struggling to stop his fall.

Finally he managed to grab a limb about 500 feet from the top and 500 feet from the bottom. He looked down and shouted, "Help! Is anybody down there?" There was no answer. He looked up and shouted, "Anyone up there?" A voice came back: "Yes, I am the Lord." The man said, "Lord, I'm about to die." The Lord said, "I will help you. First, have faith in me and turn loose of the limb and I will help you." The man looked down 500 feet, and then he looked up again and shouted, "Is there anyone else up there?"

Basketball and Religion

Bones McKinney was a delightful man. He was best known as a basketball player and coach, but he was also a Baptist preacher. He told this story on himself:

"I stopped for a traffic light. The car in front of me had a sticker on the bumper that read, 'Honk if you love Jesus,' so I started blowing my horn and continued until the driver of the car in front of me got out and walked back and shouted, 'You son of a bitch, can't you see the light is red?'"

When Bones was basketball coach at Wake Forest, his team was playing the Tar Heels in Chapel Hill. Both teams were in contention for the Atlantic Coast Conference title. Billy Carmichael was at the game, of course. He was the head lobbyist and public relations advocate for the University of North Carolina. (Among other things, he got right much credit for the Morehead Scholarships. On one occasion, I was having lunch at the Carolina Inn with Joe Hunt when Billy and John Motley Morehead came out of a private dining room. Joe said to me, "Look at Billy. He's got his right arm around Mr. Morehead's shoulder and his left hand in his pocket book.")

With seconds left to play, Wake Forest and North Carolina were tied. Then Lennie Rosenbluth sank a long shot that won the game for Carolina. Billy, a devout Catholic, went up to Bones and put his arm around him and said, "For a long time us Catholics and you Baptists have been at war with each other, but tonight a Jew won the game."

The Lost Preacher

Carl Goerch from "Little" Washington, editor of *The State* magazine and a great storyteller, tells about an itinerant preacher who
sailed his boat up and down the coast. He would stop, put up a tent
and for two or three weeks have nightly services, or "tent meetings."

On one occasion, he stopped at Ocracoke on the Outer Banks of
North Carolina. In one of his sermons, he would show charts of the
skies with the moon and stars. He would then read from the Bible
and he could show his congregation exactly where Heaven was,
based upon Biblical information. After two weeks of services at
Okracoke, he folded up his tent, put it on his boat and headed for
Hatteras.

Unfortunately, he got lost, but as luck would have it, he came
across a boat manned by two Ocracoke fishermen. He asked them
which way it was to Hatteras, and they pointed it out.

After he sailed off, one of the fishermen said to the other, "For
two weeks that preacher has been telling us how to get from
Ocracoke to Heaven, and he don't even know how to get from
Ocracoke to Hatteras."

I once asked a resident of Hatteras what they ate. He said they ate fish, and I asked if they didn't get tired of eating fish. He answered, "Oh yeah, oh yeah, but if we do, we just go over to the sound and catch some flounder."

It was the first time that I learned flounder was not a fish.

God's Little Acre

There was a very respected country preacher. When he died one of the bequests in his will was "to God one acre of land on my farm." This was a unique bequest, and the executor filed a petition asking the court for instructions. The law required that all interested parties be given notice. The sheriff had the duty of serving the notice and he did the best he could and finally wrote on the summons: "I could not find God in Anson County."

Mountaintop Religion

Once when I was at Hugh Morton's "Singing on the Mountain" affair I heard a preacher from New York make a speech in a field near the top of Grandfather Mountain. He told about taking a group of 12-year-olds on a hike to the top of the mountain when he was a young man. It was a long, laborious journey. He intended for it to be an educational trip for the children, and when they finally got to the top, he asked them, "What is bushy and has a long tail and eats nuts?"

One little boy answered, "God."

The preacher asked the boy how he arrived at that answer.

The little boy said, "I didn't figure you would make us climb this darn mountain just to talk about a squirrel."

Living the Faith

I found it very easy to become a member of a church. My remem-
brance from childhood is that every Sunday the preacher would plead
for me and others to join the church. The choir would sing the last
hymn twice, with the hope that someone would walk down the aisle.
And if you did, you were a member.

It was also easy to be a member of the church. The preacher
would tell us what we should do and what we shouldn't do. If you
didn't do what he said, they wouldn't throw you out of the church.
They would forgive you if you said you were sorry and promised to
try to do better.

As time went by, I developed some beliefs that caused me to realize that living a Christian life is hard. I was supposed to love people I
hated. I'm still working on that and it is not easy. I think there may be
a lot of truth in the saying: "Most Americans would be equally
shocked at hearing religion doubted and at seeing it practiced."

The 1960s was a time of testing for people trying to live a
Christian life. In the early days of desegregation and civil rights sit-ins
and demonstrations, what had been a way of life in the South was
being challenged and changed, and a lot of people didn't like it.

Hatred was rampant, and there were plenty of politicians ready to encourage it for their own advantage. If our way of life was being challenged, so was our commitment to our faith.

I heard of a young minister in Philadelphia who felt the call to go to Mississippi in support of the civil rights movement. People were being killed and riots were a common occurrence. He asked the ruling body of his church for a leave of absence. They asked him if he had asked the Lord what he should do. He said he hadn't, and they suggested that he talk with the Lord and they would meet with him again the following week.

At their next meeting, the young minister said, "I have talked with the Lord and He said by all means I should go to Mississippi. He said that He thought I was making a brave and Christian decision. He even said that He would go with me as far as Memphis."

Attending church regularly, teaching Sunday School, giving money to the church, not cussing or swearing or drinking liquor or gambling—this is all part of living a Christian life. But I believe a little more is expected for you to get a first-class ticket to Heaven, especially when I come across examples of people who make real sacrifices because they believe their religious convictions require it.

In the 1960s, I was teaching a Sunday School class and using a copy of the *Presbyterian Outlook* as source material, and in it I read an article that made a profound impression on me. It was a statement written by an Atlanta physician, Dr. Haywood N. Hill, who read it to his Sunday School class. (My friend Dick Phillips told me Dr. Hill had been at Davidson College when he was there.) This is what Dr. Hill said:

> *I am a Southerner. I was bred in the South, where my forefathers were slave-holders and Confederate soldiers. I was born and raised in Southern towns with their rigid racial patterns and their typical Southern prejudice. I was away from the South for a few years, but I returned to live in the South by choice, and I intend to remain here for the rest of my life. I love the South and its people.*
>
> *I like having two black arms in my kitchen and two black legs pushing my lawn mower to help take the drudgery out of living for*

myself and my family; and I like having them at a very minimum of cost to me.

I like choosing my own friends and associates and I like eating in pleasant places with well-bred people of my own race, class and status.

I like to worship in a church which is composed of my friends and equals, where I will be among my own group, racially, socially and intellectually.

I like for my children to go to school with their own kind and with other children of their own racial, social and intellectual level. I like for them to be shielded against poverty, ignorance, dirt and disease.

I like to practice medicine among intelligent, cooperative people who understand what I am trying to do for them, who are friends as well as patients and who pay their bills.

I like to live in a neighborhood composed of people of my own group who have pleasant, well-kept homes and where there is no conflict or strife.

I do not want my daughter to marry a Negro.

I like the racial status quo. I am a Southerner.

But, I am also a Christian. As a Christian I must believe that God created all men and that all men are equal in the sight of God. I must believe that all men are my brothers and are children of God and that I am my brother's keeper. I must believe that Jesus meant what he said when he commanded me to love my neighbor as myself, and when he commanded me to do unto others as I would have them do unto me. I must believe that the church is God's house and that it does not belong to me, to the congregation of Trinity Presbyterian Church or to the Southern Presbyterian Church. I must believe in the fellowship of all believers.

I am also a scientist and have devoted my life to the pursuit of objective truth. Therefore, I must know that while there are individual differences among people, there is no such thing as racial inferiority. I must know that within every group there are individuals with different potentialities and that I cannot arbitrarily classify anyone on the basis of his race or color. I must know that poverty and ignorance and isolation, call it segregation if you will, breed feelings of inferiority, frustration, resentment and despair, and that these feelings in turn lead to misery, to immorality, and to crime which, in turn, not only depress people and the groups involved but the community as a whole and the whole country.

Therefore, as a Christian and as a scientist I am obligated to act on the basis on what I know and what I believe, and not on the basis of what I like. I must live by conviction and by conscience rather than by preference and prejudice.

I must, therefore, regard every man, rich or poor, black or white, as a child of God and as a person, not as some kind of subhuman being or animal, or even as an inferior. I must try to see to it that every individual gets equal rights under the law and in politics. This applies particularly to the right of equal justice in the courts and to the right of the exercise of political privilege, that is, the right to vote. If I fear the effects of bloc voting and voting from ignorance, then I must try to see to it that every man is educated to the point where he votes intelligently.

I am obligated to pay a living wage to every man who works for me and to do my best to see that others do the same. I must accord every man the right to rise to the limit of his abilities in any job or profession, and I must make every attempt to see that no man is blocked because of his race or his social status. If any individual of any race rises to a position equal to mine, then I must accord to him the same privileges that I have and welcome him as an equal.

I must see to it that everyone has an opportunity for an education as good as my own children have. If this means, as the social scientists, the courts and the Negroes themselves believe, that that education must be the same education as my children have, then I must accept it and encourage it.

I must try to see to it that no man be humiliated and rejected because of his color. If this means that the Negro eats where I eat, sits next to me in public transportation, then I am obligated to accept it.

I must see to it that every man has an opportunity for a decent home and decent surroundings, and if this means that he will live in my neighborhood or in the house next to mine, then that is the way it must be.

If a Negro wants to worship in my church or join my church, then I am obligated to see to it that he is not only accepted, but welcomed into that church, even if it be Trinity Presbyterian Church. I must not be led by false pride to try to judge his motives for coming into that church, and I must welcome him on the same basis that I would welcome any other individual.

I must try to overlook the selfish politicians who use the Negro for their own ends, the Communist agitators who delight in stirring up racial strife, the noisy, aggressive Negro who abuses his privileges and who makes life unpleasant for me, and even the Negroes who exploit their own race.

I must overlook such irrelevant questions as which race is the further developed, which race pays the most taxes, etc., and remember the basic principles on which I am trying to act and in which I believe.

I must not only accept the efforts of the Negro to achieve his legitimate aspirations, but I must try to help him achieve them, and I believe the church must do the same if it is a truly Christian church. I must do this, even though it goes against my deepest prejudices and even though it threatens my superior and isolated position in the community, and even though it entails the risk of intermarriage.

Basically the problem is not one of what I like, but what I know to be right. I must not let my wishes determine my attitude toward my associates, my school, my church or even my own family, but if I am true to the principles which I profess, then I must act according to those principles. This, I believe. (Presbytarian Outlook.)

While I grew up a Baptist, my wife grew up a Methodist. When we married, Elizabeth played the organ in her church. It is absolutely forbidden to take an organist away from a small town church, but it was OK to take a Sunday School teacher. Anyhow, I ended up in the Methodist church. Later, the Methodists got a paid organist. After that, Elizabeth played for a while at the Catholic church and then the Episcopal church, when they lost their organist. We ended up joining the Episcopal church and have stayed there even though they, too, got a paid organist.

The Baptists think we are going down and the Episcopalians think we are going up. All I know is that we are ecumenical.

The Gideon Bible

Carl Goerch recalls he was invited to speak on one occasion in Winston-Salem. He arrived early and checked into a hotel. Having some time to spare, he decided to read the Gideon Bible usually found in hotel rooms. When he opened the book, the inside cover had written in a woman's handwriting the following:

If you are in trouble and discouraged, read Psalms 34.

If you are overcome and defeated, read John 1-9.

If you are losing confidence in man, read Psalms 37.

If you are lonesome, read Psalms 23.

If you are still lonesome, call Lisa at 833-4650.

Tired, Weary and Heavy Laden

A young Catholic boy from Philadelphia was drafted during World War II and sent to Fort Bragg, North Carolina. After a week, he wrote his mother this letter:

Dear Mama,

This is the worst place I've ever been in my life. I am already in jail. Mama, I got down here and they took everything I had away from me. They cut off all of my hair. Mama, they even took my name away from me. They just call me 281. They get us up early in the morning and keep us up late at night.

I couldn't wait for Sunday to come. I was going to sleep late and go to late Mass and just rest. But Mama, Saturday afternoon they put up a notice on the bulletin board that we got to go to church at 7 o'clock the next morning. They got us up and marched us to this church like I never been in my whole life. I was sitting there, they started playing some music and some fellow stood up, opened up a book and said, "Number 281, are you tired, weary and heavy laden?"

Mama, I stood up and said, "You are damn right I am!" And Mama, they locked me up for disturbing a religious service.

The 1960s was a time of testing for people trying to live a Christian life. In the early days of desegregation and civil rights sit-ins and demonstrations, what had been a way of life in the South was being challenged and changed, and a lot of people didn't like it. Hatred was rampant, and there were plenty of politicians ready to encourage it for their own advantage. If our way of life was being challenged, so was our commitment to our faith.

RACE AND POLITICS

The Pearsall Plan

When the U.S. Supreme Court declared in 1954 that schools seg-
regated by race were inherently unequal and therefore unconstitutional, and that all public schools would have to be desegregated,
neither North Carolina nor any other Southern State simply said,
OK, and complied. It was a traumatic challenge, and even
Southerners who knew in their hearts it was right and inevitable,
wished it had never happened and didn't know how school desegregation could be made to work in their states when the white majority was overwhelmingly opposed to it.

Some states said "never." Some advocated "massive resistance."
Some declared they would resist until every legal avenue to avoid
compliance had been explored and exhausted.

North Carolina's response was something called the Pearsall Plan.

Governor William B. Umstead appointed Thomas J. Pearsall of
Rocky Mount, a respected lawyer and former Speaker of the House,
to head a 19-member committee, including three black members,
charged with studying the situation and advising the governor on
how to proceed. Umstead died suddenly on November 7, 1954, in a
Durham hospital—the only North Carolina governor to die while in

office in the twentieth century. His successor, Luther H. Hodges, asked Pearsall and the committee to continue their work and bring him some recommendations.

The committee employed two lawyers, Tom Ellis of Raleigh and W.W. (Tee) Taylor of Warren County to study what other states were doing in response to the court decision. Ellis and Taylor began their report with these words: "North Carolina will never integrate its school system." The Pearsall committee expressed strong opposition to desegregation, which it said would destroy public support for the public schools.

In 1955, a second committee, also headed by Pearsall, recommended a constitutional amendment to allow legislation under which local school boards could suspend the operation of the public schools and, under certain circumstances, provide limited public money for the private education of children.

The plan was adopted by the legislature during a one-week special session and in the required referendum voters overwhelmingly approved the constitutional amendment. The legislature then enacted the Pearsall Plan into law.

It is astonishing in retrospect that the North Carolina response—allowing school boards to close their schools rather than desegregate—was considered moderate at the time. But it was moderate compared to the rhetoric being heard in other Southern states, and it was moderate in its effect, which was what Governor Hodges and most other state leaders wanted. The Pearsall Plan was an effort to buy some time, to provide a safety valve, to disarm the demagogues ready to pounce on the situation for political advantage. In fact, the provisions of the plan were never used by any school unit. The schools remained open and, over time, complied with the court order. Race and desegregation continued to be explosive issues in Southern politics into the 1970s.

Incidentally, the courts ruled that the Pearsall Plan was unconstitutional.

Good President?

There is an old saying that before you can be a good president you first have to be a president, meaning you have to say something that you don't believe in order to get elected. In a political campaign of Abraham Lincoln's, Douglas accused him of being a radical who favored racial mixing. I guess Lincoln was forced into saying, "I am not, nor ever have been, in favor of bringing about in any way the social equality of the white and black races. I am not, nor ever have been, in favor of making voters or jurors of negroes, nor of qualifying them to hold office, nor to intermarry with white people, and I will say, in addition to this, there is a physical difference between the races which I believe will forever forbid the two races living together on terms of social and political equality." It is a sad world in which we live. There are few heroes in the political process.

The Last Segregationist

The last significant North Carolina politician to run for office as an avowed opponent of school desegregation was Dr. I. Beverly Lake, a respected legal scholar and Wake Forest law professor. Lake was a serious but unsuccessful candidate for the Democratic nomination for governor in 1960 and 1964. He challenged the legitimacy of the Supreme Court decision and criticized the Pearsall Plan for not advocating stronger resistance to desegregation. But his approach to the issue was scholarly, and he was never a fiery segregationist in the mold of George Wallace.

Governor Dan K. Moore later appointed Lake an associate justice of the state supreme court, where he served with distinction.

In 1993, Ed Rankin and I requested and were granted an interview with Dr. Lake, then retired. We believed it would be useful and of historical interest to record the views and recollections of a man who had retained widespread respect and affection even though he could be called North Carolina's last segregationist.

Q. *Please tell us something about your background, where you were born, et cetera.*

A. I was born and raised in Wake Forest. My father was

professor of physics and mathematics at the college [then Wake Forest College, now Wake Forest University in Winston-Salem]—head of the physics department. So naturally I grew up as a Wake Forest fan. My boyhood heroes were the Wake Forest athletes of my time. It was only natural that I would attend Wake Forest College. It was my expectation in college that I would become a professor of physics and mathematics. (I have difficulty now adding and subtracting.) So I majored in college in physics and mathematics and was very fortunate to have excellent instruction. Wake Forest had a fine faculty in those days—and still does.

I knew all the faculty and they all took me under their wing and guided and directed me. However, they are not responsible for all my shortcomings, but I benefited a great deal from what they did to help me, both in and out of class. Wake Forest Law School had as its dean and founder Dr. W.T. Gulley. He was a remarkable gentleman and a fine lawyer. I don't know how I became interested in becoming a lawyer except by observing Dr. Gulley and the students of the law school. I knew them all when they were going to law school.

When I went to Wake Forest Law School, Dean Gulley was the dean, Edgar Timberlake and Bruce White were members of the faculty. It was a small faculty, but excellent in quality. I was here only a year. Back in my day, the North Carolina public schools were not as good as they are now in many respects and in many other respects they may have been better. Actually, I never graduated from high school. I just went on to college. I was 18 years old.

My father, a great scholar, said, "Now, if you want to go into law, I want you to have a good legal education. I want you to go to Harvard Law School." Which I did. My year of law school convinced me that I did want to study law. So I went to Harvard and graduated from the Harvard Law School in 1929 at age 23. There was a marvelous faculty there. Roscoe Pound was the dean.

Then I returned to Wake Forest and went to Raleigh and got a job in the law office of Smith & Joyner [Willis Smith and William T. Joyner]. They were relatively young men and I couldn't have had better instruction in practical law—or theoretical either. They were fine scholars, fine gentlemen and good lawyers. I practiced with them for three years and then decided that I wanted to go into teaching, so I got a job teaching in the Wake Forest Law School. I was the fourth man in the faculty—Gulley, Timberlake, White and Lake. After I taught awhile I attended Columbia Law School to do my graduate study in law. This led later to my earning my doctorate in 1940, when I had to write my thesis on discrimination on railroads and public utilities. It was not about racial but economic discrimination.

I returned to teaching at Wake Forest and I enjoyed teaching in the Law School, but I did not want to move to Winston-Salem when the college was relocated there. After private practice of law, Attorney General Harry McMullan hired me as an assistant attorney general and I greatly enjoyed that. I had splendid colleagues and associates there. They were splendid lawyers and fine North Carolinians.

Q. *Did you enjoy the practice of law?*

A. Yes. I did. I got along reasonably well as a practitioner. I enjoyed trial practice. Perhaps I enjoyed appellate practice more—writing briefs and arguing cases.

Q. *Do any lawyers stand out in your mind as being great lawyers in North Carolina?*

A. Colonel Joyner and Willis Smith were my heroes. Harry McGalliard was an able lawyer.

Q. *How about Jim Pou of Smithfield?*

A. He was a great lawyer and a very fine gentleman.

Q. *Is the day of the general practitioner of law gone? There seems to be just specialization of the law. The country lawyer is somewhat like the country doctor.*

A. I have been out of the practice of law for some time. My

impression is that the day of the old general practitioner has to a large degree passed—when a lawyer would open his own office and the clients would come to him. I enjoyed the general practice of law. I did not do much criminal practice. My work was mostly civil practice. At Smith and Joyner I did trial practice for insurance liability companies and so I fell into that type of trial practice. I don't know how I got started in public utility practice but I represented a number of these companies, including Carolina Power & Light.

Q. *How did your interest in politics develop, beginning as a young man?*

A. That has been so long ago I don't know the answer to that question. I guess it developed as a by-product of my legal practice. There was then—and to some degree true today—a close relationship between the bar and politics.

Q. *Were you born a Democrat?*

A. Yes—and I am still a registered Democrat. I was born and raised a Democrat. Back in my days, it was sort of expected of white people that they belong to the Democratic Party. So I just drifted into the Democratic Party. My paternal grandfather was a Baptist minister up in northern Virginia, and pastor of a Baptist church there for fifty years. We spent all our summers with him in northern Virginia, traveling there by Seaboard Railroad. My maternal grandfather was from Kentucky. He was a member of Congress, representing his district in Kentucky for a number of terms. He was a lifelong Democratic Party leader. He died when I was a young boy so I did not have the benefit of his guidance in politics.

Q. *Someone said you couldn't pay an American a higher compliment than to say he is a politician because it means he is interested in participating in the affairs of his time. Do you agree?*

A. I think that is right. That was true when I was growing up and I think still true to some degree. I was always interested in politics.

Q. *You were born a Baptist?*

A. Yes. I didn't know there was any other way to get to Heaven.

Q. *Who are some of the people in politics who have contributed meaningfully to the state?*

A. The men who influenced me and inspired me in politics—in addition to my father who was a very fine statesman-like, scholarly politician (he never ran for office himself but was interested in government)—were Willis Smith and William Joyner. And Harry McMullan. Ralph Moody was one of my guiding heroes in politics. Ralph was a great lawyer and a great man. I thoroughly enjoyed my association with Ralph while in the attorney general's office and afterwards.

Q. [Pat Taylor] *My daddy and William Rodman were good friends. One time he invited my daddy and me and Ralph Moody on his boat. Moody called me the day before we were to leave and said, "Does Judge Rodman drink whiskey?" I said, "I don't know, but I suspect he does." Moody replied, "I didn't want to get trapped on that boat for three days and no whiskey."*

A. Ralph knew what it tasted like.

Q. *What about North Carolina judges? Those with good legal minds?*

A. Walter Stacy was chief justice and a great man and lawyer William Rodman.

Q. *What about R. Hunt Parker [former chief justice of the Supreme Court]?*

A. Now, how long do you have for me to answer that question? R. Hunt Parker was one of the truly great North Carolinians, not only as a lawyer (he was excellent) but a fine man and a fine friend. He knew North Carolina about as well as anybody could. He was one of my inspiring leaders. He took me under his wing and guided my faltering footsteps as I tried to be a good judge. I was very fortunate I had remarkable friends who helped and guided and told me about my mistakes.

Q. [Ed Rankin] *Dr. Lake, Hugh Morton and I interviewed Sam Ervin [former United States Senator] shortly before he died. We asked him how he would describe North Carolina to someone from outside the state. In other words, what kind of people are we? He said that our people would follow good leadership and this loyalty has been one of the greatest attributes of our state. Do you agree?*

A. I do. I have lived elsewhere, temporarily. I went to Boston to law school for three years and I got to know Massachusetts. They had some very attractive young ladies up there. My education was not limited to the Harvard Law School. North Carolina is a state that is characterized by friendly neighborliness. Wherever I would go in North Carolina today I would be confident of being given a friendly welcome in any city or rural to settle and practice law. My first wife was a North Carolina girl. She was in the adjutant general's office. She ran the National Guard. Adjutant generals came and went but she knew them all. She led me in my devotion to North Carolina. North Carolina has always been my home. I have never wanted to live anywhere else. Campaigning across North Carolina for public office made me feel at home from Cherokee to Manteo. I love the whole state. We have a glorious history in North Carolina of public service and a well-educated people. I do not mean a multiplicity of graduate degrees but our people have common sense. This is a characteristic of the people of North Carolina. They are not swept off their feet easily by some popular campaign. When I was growing up as a Democrat you looked at someone who was a Republican out of the corner of your eye to see if he was all there mentally. I have found out that was a mistake on my part.

Q. *North Carolina, with a long history of a strong Democratic majority, has now elected two Republican governors, and appears to be a two-party state. Why do you think this has happened?*

A. The first national campaign that interested me was the Al Smith campaign for president. Rightly or wrongly, I was right much a prohibitionist. Al Smith was leader of the moderate use of alcohol. The 18th Amendment had been passed and became a part of the United States Constitution before I got grown. North Carolina was a dry state before the 18th Amendment. So I grew up believing that advocates of alcohol were wrong. For that reason, the Democrats under Al Smith were regarded as the party of liquor interests. Being brought up in the Baptist church, I didn't think that was good. My father did not use alcohol. He wasn't a fanatic, by any means, but we had no whiskey in our home, for example. My grandfather, the Baptist minister, was a strong temperance advocate. I grew up thinking that prohibition of the sale of alcohol was good law—and I still think so. I don't think a man is bad because he takes a drink of whiskey every night. That is his personal business. But it is an unwise habit to develop.

Q. *What about Al Smith's Catholicism?*

A. That didn't make much difference to me. It did to a lot of people.

Q. *Didn't it make a big difference with many Baptists?*

A. Yes, it did. Between the two, Al Smith's Catholicism had more to do with his defeat than his tolerance of alcohol. Wake Forest has always been, even when I was a little boy, a tolerant, broadminded community. It is the influence of the college. Dr. Billy Poteat, who was the president of the college, was a leader of the North Carolina temperance group, and he guided us in that direction. Dr. Billy was a great man. One of the things about old Wake Forest, which influenced me tremendously, was the friendliness of the scholars. Wake Forest was a Baptist college and the college was the center of our life and education. We had truly in the old Wake Forest College a remarkable selection of scholarly gentlemen. I would go along the street as a little boy and I walked down the street with the head of the department of chemistry, modern languages, et cetera. And we would talk about everything. I grew up under the influence of tolerance and broadmindedness.

Q. *Do you think it was a mistake for Wake Forest to move to Winston-Salem?*

A. No. Wake Forest has become a great university in Winston-Salem. The Reynolds wanted it in Winston-Salem. They moved Wake Forest to Winston-Salem more for Winston-Salem than for Wake Forest College. I hated to see Wake Forest College move to Winston-Salem because this was my home, but probably the move was wise.

Q. *What were your views, and your father's views, on dancing at Wake Forest College?*

A. My grandfather was a Baptist minister and Baptist ministers in those days were opposed to dancing. My father did not dance but was not rabid on the subject of dancing. He thought it was perfectly all right for people to dance. My two brothers and at least one of my sisters learned to dance, and I learned to dance and that was all right. We did not have dancing in our house and no big dances in the community of Wake Forest. When I went off to law school, I learned to dance and that was all right. Nobody at Wake Forest—and I mean this seriously— thought that I was headed to hell because I learned to dance.

Q. *Did not Dr. Billy Poteat lead the opposition in the North Carolina general assembly to proposed legislation to forbid the teaching of evolution in the public schools?*

A. That is right. Dr. Billy Poteat was a leader and the entire Wake Forest faculty followed and supported his leadership.

Q. *Would you approve or disapprove of a lottery in this state?*

A. I do not believe in lotteries. I think it is bad. I think it is bad economically. I have never been a gambler myself. I don't think gambling is one of the major sins of the world. But I think it is a foolish habit. Gambling is dangerous because it tends to create a desire to get rich without doing anything worthwhile.

Q. *Would you equate it somewhat with drinking alcohol?*

A. Oh, yes. When I went to Harvard Law School there was

nothing unusual for people to drink. I lived in a rooming house at Cambridge and many of the young men who lived in that house drank. I do not recall any one of my associates who was a habitual drinker, and I don't recall that they got drunk. But I learned that a man could drink without being a bad man.

Q. *Did you smoke?*

A. Oh, yes. I quit some years ago for reasons of health, but my father was an inveterate pipe smoker. The first thing he did when he got up was to fill up his pipe and put it in his mouth. He smoked all day except when he was teaching.

Q. *Do you have any comments on the controversy in the Baptist Church between the so-called fundamentalists and moderates?*

A. I guess if I tried to characterize myself—which I try not to do—I would consider myself as a moderate fundamentalist. I am a fundamentalist both in religion and politics. I believe there are certain principles that should guide a person. My grandfather, the Baptist preacher, was a staunch fundamentalist. Yet he was tolerant and broadminded. He had many, many friends who were not as deeply interested in theological matters as he was. He got along with all of them.

Q. *You said you were a fundamentalist in politics. Would you explain that, please?*

A. I was brought up a Democrat. I grew up in the latter part of the Reconstruction era. So Republicans were looked upon as a mixture of moderate intelligence and not too strong character. The Democratic Party, like the Baptist Church, was something that nice people belonged to. I grew up that way. Now when I went off to law school I quickly learned by association with some fine friends who were Republicans (my roommate was a Republican from Baltimore) that Republicans dressed just like ordinary folks and had many of the same characteristics. Naturally my law school friends and I talked politics and I found out that they were very smart people. This was the Al Smith era and I was not an Al Smith devotee. I thought then and think now that Al Smith was a great man, and a man of ability and character. But I did not agree with a lot of his ideas, particularly his attitude on prohibition. I found you could not distinguish Democrats and Republicans solely on the grounds of good and evil.

Q. *Did you not find a relationship between Republicans and many Southern Democrats, especially in Congress?*

A. Yes. If you disregard party, and choose between conservative and liberal, I would have been a conservative. So I became a conservative Democrat—and still am.

Q. *What fundamental changes have you seen in the American way of life, American law and American politics that you think have been good or have been bad?*

A. I don't think you can distinguish between Democrats and Republicans on the basis of good or evil, or on the ground of wisdom and stupidity. By nature I am a conservative, and I think the old Southern Democrat philosophy of government was sound—a conservative government based on loyalty to the Constitution of the United States, and resistance to change—unless there is some good reason to change.

Q. *Do you believe that the Rural Electrification program was a good program?*

A. I don't think I remember what I thought before but I think I would say yes. I think that it is one of the good things the Roosevelt wing of the Democratic Party did—electrification of rural areas. To bring the rural people of the state and nation up in material resources. REA was probably the center of it.

Q. *What about Social Security?*

A. The general idea of Social Security was fine. I thought then and think now that about 60 percent of Mr. Roosevelt's program was designed to help him and his group politically. He was trying to appeal to things that were popular, and the underprivileged people could vote just like the privileged and count just as much. And there were more of them. I do not think Franklin Roosevelt was divinely inspired. I think Franklin Roosevelt was a self-seeking politician. He used the Depression and obvious needs of people to appeal to them and to hold out to the underprivileged masses, particularly our colored people who were depressed financially and otherwise. He held out to them promises—more implied than expressed—that if you just elect me everything is going to be all right. And that's what he was aiming at—being re-elected. I was opposed—and still think it was a bad idea—to multiple terms of office for presidents. I thought the old practice of two terms was enough.

Q. *What about the governor of North Carolina?*

A. I don't know how to answer that one, particularly. I think one term is probably enough—for most. I do not like arbitrary classifications. I think it is a mistake to say nobody can be governor but one term. I think that is something that ought to be left to the people. But I think in general it is best to have no re-elections. If a man becomes governor, and knows from the beginning that he has four years and can't be re-elected, his policies are not shaped primarily toward his re-election. Now if he is a Democrat, he wants his successor to carry on his policies. But I think that one term, as a general practice, is wise.

Q. *As a man with such wide experience, how do you feel about the future of North Carolina—and our nation?*

A. I am a great believer in the future. I think that North Carolina—and I'm trying to be serious and conservative as I can be—is the finest part of the world in which to live. And I'm glad that my son and my grandchildren live in North Carolina. I think we have a great future in North Carolina. I do not think that everything good has already happened. And that basically is based on my belief in God. I believe in God. I believe there is a God and that He is concerned with us today—and guides and directs us. And I think that if we have faith in Him and follow His leadership, and seek to find out what His will is, I think that the future 50 years from now is beyond our comprehension.

How good it is going to be. I believe in the future based on the conservative appreciation of what we already have. We have a great history in North Carolina, a great history of progress, and I think we will continue to do that. North Carolina of my great-grandchildren's young adulthood is going to be a whole lot finer than North Carolina today.

Q. *When the Supreme Court of the United States handed down the Brown decision requiring public school integration, did you believe that decision was right from a legal standpoint?*

A. No, I did not.

Q. *Have you changed your opinion on that?*

A. No, I can't say that I have. I thought then and still think that race pride is a desirable thing. We ought to develop, as much as possible, a pride of our colored people in being colored people. There is no reason why they shouldn't be. It is not easy to do. Now, don't misunderstand me. I am white man. And I'm glad that I'm a white man. I would be horribly mortified—and I don't know what I would do—if one of my great-grand-daughters were to marry a Negro. I think that would be horrible. I believe in race pride and race separation. But race pride does not mean depressing another race. They should be encouraged to go forward—and do as much as they can. But I do not think that tolerance requires breaking down all racial distinctions. I believe in race.

Q. *From a practical standpoint, do you think the integration of our schools over the last 25 to 30 years has done anything to break down racial pride?*

A. I don't know how to answer that. I don't think I could help but have some tendency in that direction. In the first place, I know and you know that—as I intimated a while ago—the Negro race, the Chinese race—either one (and when I say race I'm not just talking about Caucasian and Negro) I'm talking about Chinese and the rest of them. I would not want my grandchild to marry a Chinese because they have a different background, traditions and customs. I don't think when you mix people up, you can help to have some tendency to break down consciousness, I would say, of racial heritage. I believe in heritage. I also think there is a difference between white people. If this is a person with a French background, or a Spanish background, he probably has a different outlook on life than one who has my background. I think naturally—I'm a human being—we have a tendency to feel that my own background is good and I want to preserve it. That doesn't mean I'm intolerant necessarily of others. And I think that of the very, very fine heritage of Italian, Spanish and so on. But I think they are different heritages from the Anglo-Saxon.

Q. *Dr. Lake, I've often thought that it was somewhat of a paradox that on Sunday morning millions of Americans go to Christian churches and worship a Jew, and then go out Sunday afternoon and play golf at a country club that won't let a Jew in.*

A. I don't carry racial pride and heritage that far. I have no objection to belonging to a club that has Jewish members so far as that is concerned. I think the Jewish background, the Jewish heritage is different from mine and I think mine is better. I would prefer that my descendants marry Caucasian gentiles. But I would not be horrified if one of my great-grandsons married a Jewish girl. I have known many, many marvelous, fine Jewish women and Jewish men. And I respect them. And I have no animosity toward them because they are Jews. I am very, very opposed to stirring up hatred between different segments of society. Now that is what destroyed Hitler. The Jews didn't destroy Hitler. Hitler destroyed himself by teaching people to hate Jews. That won't do. I do not believe—and I have practiced my belief—in group hatred whether it is racial, political or whatever. I know from experience that the Republicans are just as fine, Christian Americans as any Democrats could possibly be. I think they are wrong in many respects, although I am more and more inclined to be a Republican myself. My son is a Republican. So I have no animosity toward Republicans.

Q. *What motivated you to run for governor of North Carolina?*

A. That has been a long time ago. There were many things. I thought that the Democratic Party under the leadership of the Al Smith group was exceedingly liberal, and I wanted to bring North Carolina back from that philosophy. I thought we had a great North Carolina in those days—and still do—still think so—and I wanted to build on that foundation. And I thought that the Democratic Party in that day under the leadership of Al Smith and his group in New York were too liberal. They did not appreciate our heritage as they should have, and I felt like there was too much emphasis in those days of breaking down the distinctions between the states. I am a Southerner. I am proud of being a Southerner. That doesn't mean that I am antagonistic to people from the state of Washington. But I think that we have a fine government—the philosophy of government—and I wanted to emphasize that.

Q. *Someone said you got more votes for a dollar spent than anyone who ever ran for governor. Any comment?*

A. I guess that's true because I didn't have many dollars. We had very little money, as you know. Now my campaign—in spite of the fact that there is the tendency to characterize it otherwise—I am confident in saying this—was not based on racial discrimination. I did not believe in the integration of our schools. I thought it would damage our children by causing them to diminish their admiration of their heritage. I felt that our heritage as white North Carolinians was the thing we based our North Carolina upon. And we should hold on to that and build on that—and that North Carolina heritage. I know this is true. North Carolina heritage was not based on racial hatred and animosity. I do not recall any suggestion by responsible white North Carolinians that we ought to downgrade the Negroes or oppress them. Everybody in my group felt that we ought to do what we could to motivate the Negroes to rise to a high level economically and socially—but not necessarily to intermix. Now how to draw that line—here are differences of opinion.

Q. *Dr. Lake, we did not put as much money in black schools as we did in white schools.*

A. And we should. We should have put as much. Had I become governor, I would have advocated doing everything that we could to improve our black schools because our black children, when I was growing up, did not have the educational opportunities I had. And Lord knows I didn't have very many. You cannot imagine what the public schools were like when I went to them. I would have advocated and I did advocate improving the educational opportunities of our black children—and the business opportunities of our black people. There are many of those things that have been done that I agree with—I think they are fine. But I do not think that social integration is an indispensable prerequisite of that.

Q. *After you lost your race for governor, and were appointed to the Supreme Court of North Carolina by Governor Dan Moore to replace William Rodman, how many years did you serve on the bench?*

A. About ten years, I think.

Q. *Did you find the court satisfying work?*

A. Oh, yes. I thoroughly enjoyed my life on the court. I felt like we accomplished a good deal. I had some delightful associates on the court.

Certainly with several other people on the court you prefer one over the other, and you have differences of opinion on legal questions and otherwise, but I say without hesitation that all the people with whom I served on the court were highly intelligent, respected people and I thoroughly enjoyed working with them. We had sharp differences of opinion about the law. We did not have any personal animosities on the court when I was there.

Q. *What did you think of Judge Susie Sharp?*

A. Susie Sharp was one of the finest ladies I have ever

known. She's brilliant. Susie and I used to talk a lot about legal matters. I have the highest regard for Susie. It is not just respect—which it is—it is admiration. Susie has a brilliant mind and is just as tolerant as can be.

Q. *What about Joe Branch?*

A. Well, Joe was one of my students at Wake Forest. Joe and I have been long personal friends since those days. Joe Branch is a great judge.

Q. [Pat Taylor] *You know the Frenchman who came over here about 150 years ago, saying he was looking for the greatness of America. He concluded by saying America is great because it is good, and if it ceases to be good it will cease to be great. Do you agree?*

A. I think that is right. Now when we say America is good and he said that America is good, it did not mean that Americans never do anything wrong because I am an American and I know I frequently do many things that are wrong. America is basically kind, basically neighborly and basically tolerant. These are characteristics of America.

Q. [Pat Taylor] *I was involved right much in the revision of our judicial section of the constitution, and Mr. Edwin Gill [then state treasurer] went all over North Carolina campaigning against the appointment of judges. He was adamant on it. We could not have gotten the revision passed if we had left in the appointment of judges. On the other hand, when the electorate of North Carolina almost elected a fireman to the Supreme Court, you know that people do not take an interest in all these offices that they should.*

A. They don't know what the office requires.

Q. [Pat Taylor] *Each one has an equal vote.*

A. I know that. I know that. I ran for political office.

FRIENDS, CHARACTERS AND HEROES

Hiking the Appalachian Trail

One winter night Dick Phillips and I were talking about one thing or another and decided we would like to take a hike on the Appalachian Trail the next summer. This was a year or two before Terry Sanford ran for governor. Dick, who was practicing law with Terry at the time, brought him along.

There is a road from Bryson City to Gatlinburg, Tennessee that crosses the Smoky Mountains at Newfound Gap. The three of us were going to take three days, hike 10 miles a day, and have someone lined up to meet us at the end of our hike. We thought we could walk 10 miles in two hours, no big deal. So we took to the trail and leisurely took our time, reached Newfound Gap about noon and headed out in a northeasterly direction.

To show how little I knew about hiking, I carried a copy of *Pickwick Papers,* which I imagined I would read along the way. We planned to walk for 50 minutes and rest for 10 minutes. Before the day was over, we were taking 50 steps and resting 10 minutes. It was all up and down. With a 10-pound pack on each back, we had no idea how tired we would get.

Finally, about 10 P.M., we came to an Appalachian Trail shelter where there was a spring for water and some cover from the weather. We were exhausted and ready to sleep, but we did prepare and eat some supper. Meanwhile, we had been warned that black bears were known to raid hikers' food supplies, so we took all our food and hung it up a limb of a nearby tree. We also carried tomato juice in individual cans—not a good idea for hiking because of the extra weight—but we put the cans in the spring to keep cool. I took a pint of whiskey because I thought it might be needed for medicinal purposes.

About two A.M., we were awakened by a terrible crash. A bear had invaded our little camp, stood on his hind legs, broke the tree limb, grabbed our bag of food and took off across the hill. He took everything we had except my pint of whiskey. There was nothing to do except go back to bed.

The next morning we surveyed the damage. Even our tomato juice was gone. The bear had bitten into each can and sucked out the tomato juice. Without food or tomato juice, we did the only sensible thing—we divided my pint of whiskey. Without food, we obviously could not go on so we reluctantly retraced our steps back to where we had had started our ill-fated adventure.

The next year, Dick Phillips and I, without Terry Sanford, spent three days walking from Clingman's Dome to Fontana Dam. I enjoy the concept of hiking but the reality of hiking is something else. Doctors and health providers strongly urge other people to take exercise for their health. To me, it is boring and tiresome. I have made resolutions to take exercise the first thing in the morning. When I do this, I am tired all the rest of the day. When I wait until the end of the day, I am too tired. When the doctor says to take exercise, it is the same thing as when he says, "Take your medicine."

But hiking on the Appalachian Trail with a good friend is another matter. Perhaps it makes the medicine go down more easily. Dick Phillips had Abercrombie and Fitch hiking boots and six pairs of socks. He washed and changed his socks religiously each day. I had a pair of brogans I think I had in the U.S. Marine Corps and one pair of socks. The shoe sole came loose and was flapping all the time. But we walked 35 miles in three days across very rough terrain. At one rest stop on top of Old Thunderhead, I apparently left my wristwatch. When I discovered this sometime later down the trail, Dick urged me to go back and get it. No way—not for any watch. So we went on and arrived at Fontana Dam at five P.M. There was no car or transportation waiting or available.

We then met a young Austrian couple, also hikers, who were going in the reverse direction, and we walked across the dam with them. They asked where they could buy some alcoholic beverages—wine, beer or liquor. Dick and I explained the North Carolina system of sale and consumption of alcoholic beverages, and suggested that if the couple would drive us to the next county they might find something alcoholic to drink. The truth was none of these mountain counties allowed legal sale of alcoholic beverages, but we needed a ride.

After several fruitless trips to nearby towns, we suggested Bryson City (where our car was parked). They finally drove us there—40 or 50 miles—to find another dry county. Meanwhile, we were feeling guilty and I whispered to Dick that we had to find something for them to drink. Dick agreed. He said there is always a way to get whiskey. Just ask a cab driver. So we hired a local cab in Bryson City, explained our need and the cab driver took us out of town, down a little mountain road, pointed across a stream at a small house, and said, "You can buy it over there."

So Dick Phillips, distinguished lawyer, law school dean and now U.S. Fourth Circuit judge, crossed the little footbridge and knocked on the door of the darkened house. A dim porch light came on, the door opened slowly and he made the transaction. We gave the bottle to the Austrian couple with many thanks for their generous assistance to us. Dick and I, driving home, wondered what the young couple must have thought of us and our search for something to drink in the mountains of western North Carolina.

More About Dick Phillips

Some time later, I went to see Dick Phillips when he was dean of the Law School at UNC-Chapel Hill. He said that one of the questions on the law school application is: "Have you ever been convicted of a violation of the law, other than a traffic offense? If so, explain." One young man acknowledged that he had been convicted of a violation. His explanation: "I was convicted of indecent conduct. Last summer I was at Myrtle Beach at the Pavilion doing a new dance that the police officer obviously was not familiar with." Dick said he was going to accept the young man.

Dick also recalled a story about my father, who had served as lieutenant governor and as a leader in the Democratic Party. During a presidential election, my father was making a political speech in Scotland County, where Dick had grown up. My father was bearing down on how Roosevelt got the country out of the Great Depression. He said, with emphasis, "Those were hard times for all of us." He turned to Edwin Pate, from a very wealthy family, and said, "Weren't they hard times, Edwin?" To which Edwin replied, "They sure were." Dick Phillips said everyone in the audience had some trouble not laughing.

The High Sheriff of Richmond County

Raymond Goodman, the high sheriff of Richmond County, was a great public servant and a great politician. He served there for many, many years. While talking with me one day, Goodman smiled and said he was going to write a book about his many experiences as sheriff of Richmond County.

"I'm going to make $100,000 out of it," he said. "I am not going to publish it," he explained. "All I'm going to do is write it and show it to about a half dozen people in Richmond County. I believe they will pay me $100,000 not to publish it."

Coach Dean Smith

I had a friend who was a successful high school basketball coach in a large city. Many years ago he called me and asked if I knew Dean Smith. The coach said he had a high school senior who was being recruited by some 20 colleges, but not by UNC-Chapel Hill. The coach thought his player would be interested in going there.

I assured my friend that I did know Dean Smith well enough to call him about a good recruit, and I followed up with a call. Coach Smith said, "I know the player you are talking about, but if I were to recruit him, it would be as point guard, and I have already recruited a point guard for this year; however, your friend has a junior in whom I am very interested."

One year later Coach Smith called, reminded me of his interest in the talented player who was now a senior and said, "I'm going to see him next week." It was obvious that Smith knew all the good players who were seniors, but also knew the talented sophomores and freshmen. He asked me about my coach friend.

"Sometimes the coaches get involved in the recruiting and ask for things we cannot do," he said.

I told him the coach seemed to be a fine man in all my dealings with him.

Dean Smith wrote me after his visit that "the situation would not be what we would like and we will not recruit this player. We do think he is probably the best student athlete in the United States this year."

While I may have read something into it that is not there, I believe that Dean Smith turned down what he thought was the best player in the country because, in some way, he would have violated his principles. Both of the young men involved in this story went to the same college and the last one went to the NBA.

General George C. Marshall

When General George C. Marshall, Chief of Staff of the U.S. Army during World War II, later Secretary of State and author of the Marshall Plan, retired, he and Mrs. Marshall spent their summers at their home in Virginia and his winters in Pinehurst. I ran across a letter from him to my father that read as follows:

> *Dear Mr. Taylor,*
>
> *I very much appreciate your invitation to speak to the Wadesboro Rotary Club. I have only been here six weeks and have had many requests to speak to civic clubs. If I accept one, I will do nothing except speak to civic clubs for the rest of my life. I thank you, however, for the invitation.*

The letter was personal, signed by the general. You knew he was a fine gentleman.

Senator Claude Currie and Revenue Sharing

When Richard Nixon was president, I was lieutenant governor and presided over the state Senate. President Nixon wanted Spiro Agnew, then vice president, to be invited to speak to the North Carolina General Assembly in support of Nixon's program for revenue sharing. The gist of the program was that the federal government would share its wealth with the states. All that was needed was a resolution endorsing the idea, since the U.S. Congress would have to enact it.

I wasn't much in favor of extending the invitation, mainly because it took too much time away from the work of the legislature, but everybody thought it was the polite thing to do, so Vice President Agnew came and made a nice talk. Then a resolution of support was introduced and there was a lively debate. A large majority of the senators were Democrats and opposition arose because they didn't want to do anything that would help the Republicans. Debate went on for a number of hours.

Finally, the lovable Senator Claude Currie came up to me and said, "All of this reminds me of the story of the man who was walking down the street and met a friend who said to him, 'Bill, would you lend me $10 until Saturday?' Bill said, 'I'm sorry, Joe, but there are three reasons I can't. Number one, I don't have $10 and . . .' and before he could continue, Joe said, 'I'd just as soon not hear the other reasons.'"

The good Senator said he didn't think the federal government had any money to share and, besides, they would just be sending back a part of what we sent them.

Dr. Albert Coates

Two of my favorite people were Dr. and Mrs. Albert Coates of Chapel Hill. He was the founder and director of the Institute of Government there.

When I think of longevity of life, I always recall this story about Dr. Coates. Dr. Coates grew up on a farm in Johnston County, and he and Mrs. Coates never had but one child and that was the Institute of Government. He was a hard worker, a visionary and always thought his greatest accomplishments lay before him, even at age 90.

Suddenly, and uncharacteristically of him, he told his wife one Saturday morning, "Maybe we ought to think about buying a cemetery lot." Mrs. Coates thought that might be a good idea, and they drove out to a perpetual care cemetery near Chapel Hill. As they were being shown around by a young salesman, Dr. Coates pointed to a lot and asked, "Young man, how much is that lot?"

The reply: "$1,500."

Whereupon, Mr. Coates exclaimed, "Good God Almighty, boy! You could buy a farm in Johnston County for $1,500."

The salesman said, "But, Dr. Coates, it's not just the lot you are buying. For $1,500 you get the lot and we agree to look after it forever."

Dr. Coates responded, "Boy, I'm not planning to be out here but for three days."

Jesse Helms

Jesse Helms has been a force in North Carolina for some 50 years. He came from Monroe, North Carolina. At one time, he was executive secretary of the North Carolina Bankers Association and was well respected. His rise to prominence came when he went to work for A.J. Fletcher, who was the owner of WRAL-TV in Raleigh. Jesse became executive vice president and vice chairman of the board. His daily program, *Viewpoint,* was widely watched by people in the station's viewing area.

He was the ultimate in conservatism. Communists, civil rights advocates and liberal college professors were assailed unmercifully and his audience loved it, and it was his springboard for his election to the United States Senate in 1972.

I never voted for Jesse and did not agree with his over-aggressive, 100 percent right-wing philosophy, but I have always liked him, often agreed with what he said, and admired that he stood up for what he believed. His votes against the position of Republicans, including the President of the United States, if he didn't believe in their positions, were laudable. He has been a godsend for Wingate University, which he attended, in his home county of Union, and has brought well-known dignitaries to speak there.

The following is taken from a telecast that he gave in April 1970, and is a good example of the editorial style his audiences appreciated so much:

> We had a telephone call the other morning from Mr. Michael Straight, deputy chairman of the National Endowment for the Arts in Washington, D.C. Mr. Straight is a very pleasant gentleman; he stated that he had become deputy chairman of his organization in November of last year.
>
> His call was in connection with this station's editorial of April 14 which had made mention of an award given by the National Endowment for the Arts (we had said that the National Foundation for the Arts had given it), an award of $750 for a "poem" submitted by Aram Saroyan. The "poem" consisted of one word, which in fact was not a word. It consisted of seven letters, 'L-I-G-H-G-H-T.' That was it; that was all there was to it.
>
> And for that, we commented, Mr. Saroyan was awarded 750 of the taxpayers' dollars. Mr. Straight of the National Endowment for the Arts advises that we were in error. The award was not for $750; it was for only $500, he said, and that's all that Mr. Saroyan received for his one-word poem. Moreover, $500, Mr. Straight mentioned later in a letter to us, is "the standard rate for poems published in a book called The American Literary Anthology." And, added Mr. Straight, The American Literary Anthology was founded for the purpose of bringing young writers, whose works are published in small magazines, to a larger public. It has been widely praised in the press.
>
> He said, "Of the 158 works published in the first three volumes, only two have been criticized." And that, Mr. Straight says, "surely is a fair proportion."
>
> No argument here about that, at the moment, at least. But, as we reminded Mr. Straight later in a second telephone conversation, our reference had been limited to the $500 prize, as it turned out to be, for a seven-letter non-word "poem." Would Mr. Straight explain the meaning of the, er, "poem?" He laughed. "It doesn't make any sense to me, either," he said.

Dr. Leo Jenkins

Dr. Leo Jenkins, regarded by some as a New Jersey carpetbagger, saw the political potential at East Carolina Teachers College (now East Carolina University) in Greenville. And he convinced many Democrats in eastern North Carolina to believe his message: "No one cares about eastern North Carolina but Leo Jenkins and ECTC. Support me and I'll take you to the Promised Land."

President John Messick had resigned in disgrace, and ECTC faced a dismal, uncertain future. The school and its alumni and other supporters responded eagerly to Jenkins' promises. After he had won approval for the ECU Medical School, Leo told me, "Now that I have my medical school, I'm going to get me a law school."

I responded, "Leo, you fooled all the people out there into thinking you were going to put a doctor in every little town in eastern North Carolina, but if you think you are going to get political support for putting a lawyer in every town in eastern North Carolina, you better have another thought coming."

That was the last I heard about a law school at ECU.

My Friend, Walon Green

Almost 50 years ago a nice looking gentleman walked into my law office. He looked as if he needed a contract or a deed or a will. To my surprise, he said, "My wife [not his first wife] and I got into a fight on US 74 near Peachland, and a state highway patrolman passing by saw the fight and charged us with disturbing the peace. There were no injuries and we've made up. We were both drunk and do you think you can get the charges dropped?"

Under those circumstances, I thought that I could and I did.

The man was Walon Green, and he and I became good friends. I had much to learn about this fascinating man. He said he was born in Weldon, N.C., and that his father was a lawyer who had at one time invested in the Broadway play, *Tobacco Road*, which had been a big success. Walon had inherited from his father a hotel in Weldon, which he still owned.

It seems that Mr. Green was an aviator in World War I and had flown with Eddie Rickenbacker, the best known WWI pilot and ace. At that time, Rickenbacker was president of Eastern Airlines. Walon said that for the last 15 years he spent his winters in Florida and his summers in New York City. He was a friend of many famous people, including Ernest Hemingway and Damon Runyon.

He had grown tired of his lifestyle, and on his return to New York that spring, he had spent a night in Charlotte, saw an advertisement in the Charlotte newspaper of a farm for sale at Peachland and that's how he got to North Carolina. Mr. Green said he had been married a time or two and that his present wife, with whom he had the altercation, had parted amicably. He said he had one child by his first marriage, and that his first wife, Virginia, was married to a songwriter who had written, among other hit songs, "Pennies from Heaven." He said his son was coming to live with him and attend Wingate College.

Mr. Green, a skilled storyteller, said that a whale washed up on Miami Beach and a tugboat was dispatched to haul the carcass several miles out to sea. Meanwhile, Ernest Hemingway and some friends were out boating and drinking and decided to ride out and see the whale. When they arrived, sharks were eating the whale and there must have been several dozen participating in the feast. Hemingway drove the boat up alongside the whale and one of the drunken passengers decided to climb up on the carcass. After managing to get on top of the huge animal, the drunk's feet slipped out from under him and he plunged down into the ocean among the feeding sharks. Apparently the sharks liked whale meat better than human because the fallen man was able to climb back in the boat unharmed.

Well, to be perfectly frank, it wasn't that I thought Mr. Green was making all of this up, but I had serious reservations as to how much was exaggeration until several things happened that changed my mind.

First, we were having dinner with Mr. Green and my good friend, Herman Hardison. Herman mentioned that he needed to go to New York City that week, wanted to fly Eastern Airlines, but could not get a reservation. Mr. Green said he would call Eddie Rickenbacker, and he did and Herman got his tickets the next day.

Second, my sister, Caroline, a pianist, was studying in New York under an elderly, well-known German piano teacher. After about a year, Dr. Friedburg wrote my parents and told them that my sister was ready for a Town Hall recital. This was exciting news for my father, mother and the family. In life, however, very few things are free. My father discovered that he would have to rent Town Hall for the evening. This would guarantee that my sister's recital would be reviewed by three leading newspapers in New York City, and this was a way to launch her musical career.

Town Hall would put the event on the marquee and the ticket office would be open, but otherwise my parents could have all the tickets they wanted. They sent tickets to everyone they knew, with most going to African-Americans who had left Anson County to find better employment in New York than they could find at home. (Through the years I have been amazed to see how many of these people have been financially successful in New York, but choose to return home to Anson County when they retire. Apparently the old saying, "There's no place like home," is true.)

Walon Green rode to New York with my wife, Elizabeth, and me for the big event. We stayed at the Drake Hotel and when we checked in there was a placard on the counter: Jimmy Flood, Manager. Mr. Green said, "I know Jimmy Flood well. He used to be at the Algonquin." About that time, Mr. Flood came out and warmly greeted Mr. Green and they talked about old times.

My sister's recital was very successful. We stayed up until four o'clock in the morning waiting for the morning paper to read the reviews. They were all very good. *The New York Times* review said, in part: "Caroline Taylor, a young pianist from North Carolina with a light, sure touch and exceptional musical sensibility, gave her first New York recital last night at Town Hall. It proved to be one of the most successful debuts of the season. One factor for the success was the program. It was almost ideally suited to Miss Taylor's talents. There were no thundering warhorses. Instead, the selections were graceful, tender, often beautiful, prevailingly feminine in mood, and although nearly all were light, they all had their moments of depth."

When my father settled up with Town Hall, he learned that two people actually bought tickets. Until he died, my father said he wished he knew the names and addresses of those two people so he could send them their money back.

Finally, my father received *The Carolina Israelite*, a newspaper published in Charlotte by Harry Golden, who gained national fame for his book, *Only in America*. I was reading his newspaper one day and found that Mr. Golden had written, "Imagine my surprise, when walking down Tryon Street, I ran into my old friend, Walon Green. I knew him years ago in New York, where he was an intimate friend of Ernest Hemingway and Damon Runyon."

At this point, I knew that my friend Walon Green was for real.

His story had a happy ending. Walon remarried his first wife and they lived happily together in Florida. Their son, Walon Green, became a successful television and film producer. I saw his name recently as a co-producer of the popular television program, *Law and Order*.

Lamar Caudle

Lamar Caudle was one of the most charming, interesting persons you would ever hope to meet. He attended Wake Forest College (now University), was elected president of the student body, was graduated from Wake Forest Law School and returned home to practice law. He was what you would call a country lawyer and not overly skilled in his specialties in the law. But he was likeable and made friends easily. He was a longtime friend and supporter of U.S. Senator Bob Reynolds.

Senator Reynolds had Caudle appointed a U.S. District Attorney for the western district of North Carolina. In this capacity, Caudle came in contact with Tom Clark, who was attorney general in the Truman administration. Clark was charmed with Caudle and had him appointed an assistant attorney general in Washington and put him in charge of civil rights. This was in the early 1940s and civil rights were not a major activity of the Justice Department at that time. Lamar told me in later years that "there wasn't many civil rights and I spent much of my time talking with Thurgood Marshall (who was then head of the National Association for the Advancement of Colored People, and later a member of the U.S. Supreme Court)."

Lamar continued: "One day Thurgood said to me, 'Mr. Attorney General, you and I have become good friends and I feel close enough to you to tell you something. It doesn't matter how hard you try to say Negro, it always comes out like you are saying nigger.'

"I said, 'Thurgood, I appreciate your telling me this and I will try to change. But I want you to know that your people taught me how to talk.'"

Later Caudle was promoted to assistant attorney general in charge of criminal prosecutions. There was a man in St. Louis whose business was shoe manufacturing and the Internal Revenue Service had investigated him for income tax fraud and the IRS was recommending prosecution. At that time, the Justice Department had discretion not to indict if the health of the proposed defendant was such that a trial might result in his death. The attorneys for the shoe manufacturer sent a dozen or more letters from prominent physicians in St. Louis giving their opinion that the shoe man was in very bad health and would die if tried. Lamar had the proposed defendant sent to Walter Reed Hospital and the results came back somewhat inconclusive.

About this time, Lamar received a telephone call from Matthew Connelly, who was press secretary for President Truman, saying, "Mr. Attorney General, the president has an old friend from Missouri who is having some trouble with the IRS. As a matter of fact, he is in serious trouble and the president would appreciate any help you might give him within the bounds of propriety."

Lamar decided not to prosecute provided the man would pay all taxes and penalties, which he did.

After the fact, the shoe man's attorney wrote Lamar and Connelly expressing his appreciation for what they had done, and as a tangible expression of his gratitude he sent each one a 1/16 interest in an oil well in Oklahoma. It was of negligible value, maybe $5,000. Both Lamar and Connelly accepted the stock, but later returned it to the lawyer.

Later President Truman fired Lamar, but apparently for another reason. Lamar was a close friend of Drew Pearson, the fearless, freewheeling Washington columnist, who had written a critical review of Margaret Truman's singing. Truman wrote Pearson an angry letter and called him an SOB for his negative review. Subsequently Pearson wrote in his column of what he considered unjust treatment of Lamar. In any event, Caudle and Connelly were indicted for the crime of "depriving the Government of their best services," tried in St. Louis, in Truman's home state, and found guilty.

Lamar spent several months in a minimum-security prison in Florida. While he was serving his prison time, I wrote him a letter and he replied: "This is a nice place. They have doctors, bankers, college professors and two lawyers. The other lawyer is not very friendly so I am the lawyer for the inmates and I spend most of my time writing Writs of Habeas Corpus for my incarcerated fraternity brothers."

Lamar returned to Wadesboro a broken man. I have always thought that his conviction was a travesty of justice and that the federal prosecutors took a factual situation that could be made to look bad and destroyed a good man and his family.

Lamar had a brother, Charles, who was also a lawyer in Wadesboro. He was not the greatest lawyer, but charming like Lamar. Back in the days when lawyers weren't appointed for indigentdefendants in criminal cases, there was an unfortunate fellow charged with a number of very serious offenses that could have put him in prison forever. When he came up for trial, the judge decided to appoint him a lawyer and he saw Charlie Caudle sitting in the courtroom.

"Mr. Caudle," the judge said, "take the defendant back in the room and see what you can do for him."

Mr. Caudle said, "Your Honor, I don't think there's anything I can do for this fellow."

The judge said, "Well, I know what you are saying, but take him back there and give him the best advice you can."

Even if counsel was appointed in those days, the counsel was generally appointed about 30 minutes before the trial was to begin. I point this out in support of the Supreme Court's ruling relating to appointment of counsel.

Charlie obediently took the defendant to the adjacent room, stayed about 10 minutes and returned, leaving the defendant alone in the room. When the case was called in about 30 minutes, the sheriff went to get the defendant and he was gone. It seems there was a sturdy drainpipe near one of the windows, and the prisoner had used this means of escape.

The judge gave Charlie a piercing look and asked, "What did you tell the defendant?"

Caudle said, "Your Honor, you instructed me to give the defendant the best advice I could, and I told him if I were in his fix, I'd get out of here if I could."

After that case, bars were placed over the windows of the holding room.

Burgwyn of Northampton

Judge W.H.S. Burgwyn of Northampton County often held court in Anson County. A man of sturdy physique and courtly manner, the judge was a good jurist, a fine gentleman and the stories about him are legion. One of the classic stories involved a defendant charged with rape. The evidence was so weak that the district attorney let him plead guilty to forcible trespass. This a catchall law used where there is no exact law to fit the facts.

The prosecution witness told a perfect story about how she was raped. Then the defendant took the stand and said it wasn't that way at all. The facts were that she had offered her services for $5 and when they got through he didn't have but $2.

"That's what the fuss was about," he said.

Judge Burgwyn leaned over the bench and said, "Boy, you are sorry. By your own admission, you are guilty of receiving goods under false pretense."

That case reminds me of an old story, which is probably fiction. There was a 14-year-old boy charged with the rape of a very large mature woman. He had no lawyer and during the trial his mother suddenly stood up, pulled her son up, unzipped his trousers and took out his little penis. Then she said, "Judge, this little boy couldn't have done what this woman says he did. Look at this little thing." Whereupon the son whispered, "Mama, if you don't turn that thing loose, we're going to lose this case."

It was well known that Judge Burgwyn had a keen appreciation for a pretty girl. He was holding court in eastern North Carolina when a beautiful blonde girl was the defendant in a charge of drunk driving.

"Mr. District Attorney," the judge said, "that pretty girl would not be guilty of driving drunk."

"Oh, yes sir, Judge," the DA said. "We have a strong case against her."

The judge said, "All right, but I don't think she is guilty."

The state put on its case and it was strong. The defense did the best it could to defend the young woman. Before a case can go to the jury, the presiding judge must instruct the jury on the law involved in the case. Here is what Judge Burgwyn was quoted as saying: "Now, gentlemen of the jury [this happened at a time when women were not allowed to serve on a jury], the officer testified that the defendant had a strong odor of alcohol on her breath. Now, everyone knows that all women wear perfume and the base of perfume is alcohol, and that the officer well could have been mistaken, and what he thought was alcohol was in reality the perfume she was wearing.

"Now, gentlemen of the jury, the officer testified that the defendant was unsteady on her feet. Now, we all know that women wear high heels and, while I have never worn high heels, I am satisfied that if I put them on I would be very unsteady on my feet."

The jury promptly acquitted the defendant. Judge Burgwyn called the DA up to the bench and said, "I told you she was not guilty."

The judge lived in Northampton County, which borders Virginia. While driving in Virginia on one occasion, he was stopped by a law enforcement officer and charged with driving under the influence. Of course, considering his position in the North Carolina judiciary and his prominence in the state, the arrest received widespread attention in the news media, especially in the Raleigh *News and Observer*. When the trial was held, Judge R. Hunt Parker of the North Carolina Supreme Court went to Virginia as a character witness for the judge. The judge was acquitted of the charge, but remained upset and chagrined about the entire matter.

Not long after the trial, he was holding court in Columbus County and there was a murder trial underway. On the second day of the trial, there was an early recess and attorney Bunn Frink said, "Judge, let's you and me and John Burney [another attorney] go down to Calabash tonight and eat oysters. My wife doesn't drink and she'll do the driving."

That suited everybody and they went to Calabash, located in nearby Brunswick County at the South Carolina border. The seafood restaurant chosen by Frink was actually in South Carolina, about a mile south of Calabash. Everyone ordered oysters that turned out to be cluster oysters, which are especially difficult to open. Frink told the waiter to get someone to come and open the judge's oysters. The waiter said the restaurant didn't have anyone to open oysters.

"If you are going to eat oysters here, you are going to open them yourselves," he said.

Whereupon, Frink, a robust man with a determined manner, demanded, "You are going to get someone to open the judge's oysters!" Voices were raised and the manager was summoned. He quickly decided that he was dealing with a bunch of troublemakers, and said, "My brother is a deputy sheriff and I going to call him and have you all arrested."

By this time, Judge Burgwyn, the guest of honor, who had recently gone though the ordeal of trial by the press in Virginia and North Carolina, and did not want another trial in South Carolina, was at the door and headed for the car. So the party beat a hasty retreat, and Mrs. Frink began driving toward the North Carolina line. Judge Burgwyn pulled out a $100 bill, handed it to Mrs. Frink and said, "If you get us to the North Carolina line before that deputy sheriff gets us, that $100 is yours."

They made it.

Trial by Prosecutors and the Press

Bryan Houck has been a friend of mine for many years. He is a Christian man who would not think of breaking the law. He has been a public relations representative and lobbyist for Southern Bell (now BellSouth) for the past 30 years or more. Back in the 1960s, the office of the U.S. district attorney in Charlotte charged him with an offense that related to how Southern Bell reported its lobbying expenses. Subsequently, the charges were dropped and Southern Bell took the blame for whatever irregularities might have taken place.

I told Bryan before he was charged that if he was charged the press would say, "If convicted, he would face up to 10 years in prison." They do it all the time.

Bryan said, "If they do that and my dear old daddy and mother hear it, they will both have a heart attack."

My attention was called to this by a headline in *The Charlotte Observer* (July 16, 2002). It was over an article about the pro basketball player, Allen Iverson: "Jail time not likely though maximum sentence is 70 years, if convicted on all charges." Subsequently, I think the charges were dropped.

Edmund Harding to the Rescue

While Luther H. Hodges was governor, he had the opportunity to host a meeting of the Southern Governors Conference in Asheville. The gala opening dinner featured entertainment selected by the host state, and Hodges was delighted that Andy Griffith agreed to perform at this special event.

Forty-eight hours before the dinner date, Andy Griffith's manager called to report that Andy had a severe case of laryngitis and couldn't speak above a whisper. The governor immediately said, "Find Edmund Harding and see if he can appear in Andy's place."

Harding, who traveled widely, was found in Illinois. He was available for that Sunday night if transportation could be arranged. A friend of the governor who had a private aircraft answered this need.

Nothing about Andy Griffith's problem had been announced, and all the governors and their parties arrived in Asheville expecting to see and hear Andy. While Harding was well known in North Carolina as an after-dinner speaker and humorist, he was largely unknown to this audience of governors and their parties. He was seated alone among many at the long head table.

At the appropriate moment, Hodges explained the absence of

Andy Griffith, thanked Edmund Harding for arranging his schedule to appear, and gave Harding a warm introduction. Harding stood up to polite applause, gave the audience his broad, beguiling smile, and began with this story:

> *After waiting for over two hours, my train arrived late at night at the Roanoke station, and I boarded my Pullman car, weary and ready for my berth. I showed my ticket to the Pullman conductor, a gruff fellow, who said, "Lower six, this car. Claim your berth."*
>
> *All the berths were made and when I located lower six, I pulled back the curtain to find there two perfectly beautiful blond girls, about 19 years old. Startled, I apologized and quickly closed the curtain.*
>
> *I immediately sought out the conductor, explained my problem and asked for help. The grim conductor would only say, "You have lower six this car. Claim your berth." So I returned to lower six, cautiously pulled back the curtain and said, "Young ladies, I am Edmund Harding from Washington, N.C., a happily married man with children, a member of the Chamber of Commerce, the organist at my church, and I have the ticket to this berth. So one of you girls is going to have to get out of there!"*

The audience roared with laughter and Edmund Harding was on his way to another successful performance.

Hugh Morton and Mrs. LBJ

Hugh Morton, owner of Grandfather Mountain, is a well-known Democrat who has long ago adjusted to being a political minority in heavily Republican Avery County. Much to his surprise, Hugh was given the Avery County Man of the Year Award by the Avery County Chamber of Commerce. In his response, he said, "This is totally unexpected and all I can think to say is that I must be the first Democrat elected to anything in Avery County."

The master of ceremonies quickly rejoined, "Wait a minute, Hugh. You weren't elected. You were chosen by committee."

At another time, Hugh was invited to a big dinner in Washington and found he was seated next to Mrs. Ladybird Johnson. When she learned he was from North Carolina, she recalled that she had served on the Blue Ridge Parkway Advisory Board while the Parkway was still under construction. There had been some fellow, she said, in western North Carolina who had blocked the building of a vital link of the Parkway across Grandfather Mountain. Did Hugh happen to know him? Meanwhile, Mrs. Dan K. Moore, the First Lady of North Carolina who was seated across the table and listening to the conversation, could hardly contain her mirth. Hugh told Mrs. LBJ that she was seated next to that stubborn fellow.

He then explained the background of his family's historic battle with the Parkway officials for many years, and the victory for every-one, which resulted in the construction of the now-famous Linn Cove Viaduct along the side of Grandfather Mountain. Hugh said Ladybird Johnson recovered quickly and they parted friends.

Judge James McMillan

James B. McMillan came from Robeson County. He became a very successful lawyer in Charlotte. I had dealings with him from time to time, and always found him to be gracious and ready to understand the merits of his client as well as yours.

He was serving as president of the North Carolina Bar Association and I was in the legislature. The Bar Association was actively supporting a reform of the judicial system of North Carolina, and Spencer Bell from Charlotte was chair of a committee that recommended substantial changes that would require a rewrite of that section of the constitution of North Carolina relating to the judicial system.

This proposal was submitted to the General Assembly and failed to pass. (To submit constitutional amendments to a vote of the people required a 3/5th vote of the members of both houses of the General Assembly.) This was in 1961 and it was resubmitted to the General Assembly in 1963, and, by chance, I was chairman of the committee in the House of Representatives to receive the bill. As a result of this, I came to know Judge McMillan very well because he came from

Charlotte almost every week by virtue of his presidency of the North Carolina Bar Association. The legislation was finally approved.

Subsequent to this, Jim was appointed a federal judge for the western district of North Carolina and pursuant to federal mandate, it was required that the Charlotte-Mecklenburg school system be integrated. Jim made every effort to get the school board to come up with a plan that he thought would comply with the law. The school board was not able to do this and it fell on the shoulders of Judge McMillan to implement the law, which he did. The result was a plan that required massive busing of students throughout the school district, and Judge McMillan was ostracized, threatened and subjected to the vilest of criticism.

As I recall, the busing plan was to become effective on a Wednesday. On Monday morning of that week, Jim called me and asked if I would like to play golf with him at the Charlotte Country Club, where he was a member. I would have missed my wife's funeral rather than turn him down. He asked me whom I would like to play with, and I told him it did not matter to me, but I did suggest a friend of mind who had recently moved to Charlotte. I learned much later that he called the home of my friend, talked with his wife and said he was Judge McMillan and that I had suggested calling her husband about playing golf. The wife thought a joke was being played on her (they had three children), and she replied, "No, he cannot play. We will both be spending all day hauling children to and from school."

In any event, Jim couldn't get anyone to play and called and asked if I would get someone. I drafted my friend, Ned Hardison from Wadesboro, and he was able to get his preacher to play with us. Not a single person spoke to Jim on the day we played, and friends of mine would only give me an icy hello.

I consider Jim McMillan to have been a profile in courage.

Momma's Up on the Roof

Phil Godwin, a fun-loving legislator from Gates County and former Speaker of the House, told this classic story at a political rally.

There was a bachelor fellow who lived in eastern North Carolina and he had a cat and he loved that cat more than he would a wife and children. He wouldn't go anywhere unless he took his cat with him.

But he always wanted to sail on the *Queen Mary* to England, but cats were not allowed with passengers so he wouldn't go. His sister, who lived nearby, urged him to take the trip. "I'll look after your cat like it was a new born baby," she promised. She finally persuaded him to go and he sailed to England on the *Queen Mary*.

As soon as the ship docked, he rushed to a telephone to call his sister.

"How's my cat?" he asked.

"The cat's dead," she said.

"What!"

She repeated: "The cat is dead."

"Well, you didn't have to tell me that way," he said.

The sister said, "The cat is dead. What else could I say?"

The brother replied, "Well, you could have told me that you took the cat out for some exercise, it was a cold and windy day, and the cat got up on the roof and you couldn't get him down . . . and you finally had to call the fire department and they came with a ladder and got the cat down. The cat is okay but has a slight cold."

He continued: "Then I could have called tomorrow and asked about my cat and you could have said the cold had gotten real bad and you took him to the vet, and the vet thinks the cat will be alright.

"The third day I could have called and you could have told me that the cat's cold had gotten much worse and you took it back to the vet who diagnosed the cold as pneumonia, so he had to be kept at the hospital for further treatment. You could have said that I should know the cat is seriously ill, but the vet thinks he will recover.

"Then I could have called you the next day and you could have said, 'Darling, I hate to tell you but your cat went into a coma last night and passed away.' If you had done it that way, I could have been prepared for it . . . but just to say the cat's dead ain't the way to do it."

The sister said, "I'm certainly sorry and I didn't mean to do it wrong."

Several days passed while he was touring England, and he called his sister to see how things were going at home. He asked, "How's Momma getting along?"

His sister said, "Well, she's doing fine. Right now she's up on the roof and we can't get her down."

The Honorable Judge

For many years one of the best known humorists in North Carolina was Edmund Harding of Washington ("little Washington" he always called it), N.C. Harding traveled the U.S. giving after dinner speeches at civic clubs, church organizations and business meetings. He kept careful records of each engagement and the stories told so that if invited again he would not repeat any of his material.

He said that during the Spanish-American war his hometown raised a company of volunteers to go to Cuba and fight the Spaniards. The company left with great fanfare by train for Raleigh, but when they got there they discovered the war was over. So they returned to Washington, never having been much more than 100 miles from home.

The officer in charge was named Jones and because he was their leader he became known as Colonel Jones for the remainder of his life. Unfortunately, he also became the town bum, with his life going downhill steadily.

Finally, the town council adopted a vagrancy ordinance, and the first fellow arrested for vagrancy was Colonel Jones. He came before the local judge who tried and convicted him. Before he pronounced sentence, the judge asked the defendant to stand up.

"Where did you get that name Colonel Jones?" the judge asked. The defendant replied, "It's like that honorable before your name. It don't mean a damn thing!"

FDR

Franklin D. Roosevelt was loved in North Carolina. We thought Herbert Hoover had gotten us into the Great Depression and that FDR had gotten us out of it, but as much as he was loved by us others hated him with great intensity.

There was a Wall Street banker whose chauffeur let him out each morning in front of his New York office building. There was a newsstand in front of the building and the banker would stop at the stand, pick up a newspaper, look at the front page, put it back and never buy a paper.

After a year or so, the man who ran the newsstand said, "Mr. Morgan, every day you pick the paper, look at the front page and never buy one, and I wonder why."

The banker said, "I'm not interested in anything but the obituaries." To which the newsstand owner pointed out, "Well, Mr. Morgan, the obituaries are not on the front page." To which the banker replied, "The son of a bitch I'm looking for will be on the front page."

Another FDR story involved a small country church where a devout Republican layman was called upon to lead in a prayer. He offered this petition: "Oh Lord, we thank you for this great land we love so much, and for the wonderful men of the past who made it what it is. Men like Lincoln, Grant, Garfield, McKinley and Roosevelt . . . Theodore, that is."

Roosevelt had two close friends in his cabinet, Harry Hopkins and Harold Ickes. The two got into a terrible fuss over a policy matter and the president, who was at his vacation home in Georgia, sent for them to come down and discuss the issue.

He first called in Hopkins, who presented his opinion. The president said, "Harry, I think you are exactly right."

Ickes followed, and when he had finished, the president said, "Harold, I think you are exactly right."

After Ickes left, Eleanor Roosevelt, who was sitting in the room, said, "Franklin, how in the world could you have told both men that they were exactly right, when their views were diametrically opposed?"

The president thought for a moment and then said, "Eleanor, I think you are exactly right."

An old lady was quoted as telling her pastor: "I would be a lot better Christian if I could love the Lord as much as I hate Franklin D. Roosevelt."

THE GREATEST GENERATION?

The Train

Of what value, if any, is it to talk about old times? It is human nature to tell about our own personal experiences, often to the boredom of our audience. Why is history a required subject in schools? Is the past the prologue to the future? I'm not sure, but the past is good source material. It certainly can be dissected and analyzed.

Perhaps you cannot make things the way they ought to be unless you understand why they are the way they are; and you cannot understand why things are the way they are unless you understand the way they were.

When you play on a football team, you know when the game is over whether you won or lost and what part you played in the outcome. Life is a little more complicated than that, but we still try to keep score, individually and generation to generation. But when does one generation end and the next begin?

Life can be compared to a train ride. On the day of your birth, you board the train and you ride until the conductor tells you it is time to get off, and that would be the day of your death.

Generations overlap and are different for everyone. My generation began on April 1, 1924, and the train is slowing down. I hope it won't stop at the next station.

So far, my generation has won a lot of big games, but also lost some. The $64.00 Question (That was the grand prize on an old radio quiz show. Today, after inflation, it would be the $1,000,000 Question.) is how many games are we going to win in the next few years? If we lose too many, all generations might have to get off the train at the next station.

I do believe the history of the past is the key to success in the future. Most basic to this are fundamental principles such as love, integrity, truthfulness and unselfishness. But we must also understand human nature, and that there are different beliefs than mine, and they must be acknowledged, if not in every case accepted. So we must add to the list of fundamentals, tolerance, and we must understand, from time to time, the value of compromise.

FDR said North Carolina was the most progressive of the Southern states. I'm not sure how much of a compliment that was, but I don't disagree with it. We have produced leaders who, in times of crisis, have kept our state on a level and lawful track and kept us out of the hands of those who would advocate extreme and unlawful actions. They led the state through the civil rights revolution with dignity and a reputation for moderation and good sense.

The year I was born, our country's involvement in World War I was still a fresh memory. Then came the Great Depression, followed by World War II, then the civil rights movement, the Vietnam War, the rebellion of a younger generation, with the widespread use of illegal drugs, then an era of great individual wealth for some, prosperity for most and persistent poverty for others, environmental problems and a great religious war with terrorists around the world.

We handled some of those challenges very well, failed badly with others. On the more recent ones, the jury is still out, and probably will be when this train ride is over.

Checking the Score

There have been conflicting assessments about my generation—Americans who grew up in the Great Depression and came of age just in time to fight in World War II. The television news anchorman Tom Brokaw has written a best-selling book calling us *The Greatest Generation*. He points out that many of us grew up in poverty, in an era of panic, fear and despair in America, with shadows of aggressive tyranny spreading across the world. We went abroad and saved humanity, East and West, from fascism and its allies, and then we came home and created the freest and most prosperous nation in the history of the world. The credit may be a bit overblown, but it is also overdue.

What a contrast that is to what was being said about us just 30 years ago. In the late 1960s and early 1970s, when I was an elected state official and twice a candidate for statewide office, much of the younger generation—my children's generation—was condemning my generation as greedy and materialistic, as indifferent to poverty and hunger and racism. We were destroying the environment in our pursuit of corporate profits and personal comfort and pleasure. We were responsible for American involvement in what they saw as an unjust war in Vietnam.

In those days, I was sometimes invited to speak at college commencement exercises and I took advantage of those occasions to try to address the concerns and deflect the accusations of those idealistic young people. I admitted that our society, in our generation, had become too materialistic, but I also pointed out that we were materialistic because when we were growing up we had seen people suffering, and many of us had suffered, from material want. We had seen starving children and we had seen unemployed parents with fear and worry in their eyes. We were determined not to let that happen to us as adults, or to our children.

We were determined, I told them, "that you would have vitamins and orange juice and milk, warm clothes, a comfortable home, and good schools, and a running start at life." Because of our determination, and our materialism, I said, "You are the biggest, tallest, healthiest, brightest and handsomest generation ever to inhabit this land, and perhaps the world. You are going to live longer, suffer sickness less often, work fewer hours, earn more, see more of the world's grandeur, and have more choices about your lives' undertaking than any generation before."

But I sensed at the time that what I was saying was not what they wanted to hear. For all the sincerity of their idealism, too many of them were committed to a romantic fantasy of youthful rebellion and unwilling to make a common cause across the generation gap, or to make the compromises and do the hard, patient work necessary for constructive change. And I think that is because they did not understand and thus could not accept the way things had been before their time.

Think what might have been accomplished if we could have harnessed their energy and idealism with those of us in my generation who were almost as idealistic and a good deal more experienced and realistic. Having failed, on both sides, to do that, what then did those disillusioned, defiant and determined young people of the 1960s and 1970s accomplish? Their support was certainly useful to the cause of civil rights, but credit for progress in civil rights must go primarily to courageous African-Americans who demonstrated, lobbied, voted and went into the courts and demanded an end to racial discrimination. And the historic new legal affirmations and protections of the rights of minorities were primarily declared and enacted by white judges and white legislators of my generation.

What else? Sadly, not much. In politics, the tactics and rebellious lifestyles of those idealistic young people created a backlash that twice helped elect the antithesis of their idealism, Richard Nixon, to the presidency. And then it was President Nixon who did what those young people who despised him had wanted all along. He pulled the United States out of Vietnam and let the communists have it. History sometimes gives us such breathtaking ironies.

Saddest of all is that the social amenities of that revolution—illegal drugs and casual sex—have had such damaging social and personal consequences. Those young people who managed to survive or escape those consequences into adulthood found their idealism at best was blunted by the banal reality of ordinary living, or at worst disintegrated into cynicism. And out of that cynicism came the explosion of shameless greed and materialism of the 1980s and the scandals on Wall Street and in corporate executive offices that began then and continue today.

Thus the "generation gap" was finally bridged—not by mutual respect, or love, or cooperation in pursuit of worthy common goals, but by the younger generation's cynical embrace of the very sins for which it had once condemned its elders.

Were we, then, the "greatest generation?" By what measure? When I read that we were great because we fought and won a world war, I am reminded of something Sen. John F. Kennedy said in 1959, the year before he was elected president of the United States. A high school student in Wisconsin asked him how he came to be a war hero. He replied: "It was easy. They sank my boat." We fought the world war because Hitler's Germany was trying to bomb our mother country into submission, and Japan attacked our base at Pearl Harbor. It wasn't a choice we made. It was something we had to do. In subsequent wars, there have been controversies and some ambivalence about our role, but there was no way we could decline to fight that war.

Were we the greatest? Certainly we were better than our critical children gave us credit for in the '60s and '70s, but we have not been as good as we should have been. We will leave the world in many ways much better than we found it, but in some ways we will leave it worse.

Certainly in North Carolina, our generation contributed distinguished leadership, and we can claim significant accomplishments in response to the challenges we faced. We led the state through the civil rights revolution with its dignity largely intact. We set the stage for the transition from an agricultural economy to a manufacturing economy to a service economy.

The problem with labeling us the greatest, as much as we appreciate it, is that it suggests that we and our time were somehow discrete, that we left no unfinished business, or that everything must go downhill from here. Perhaps it would be useful to look for a moment at our failures as well as our successes, and to consider both as part of a continuum. Because of our failures, there is much work to be done. Because of our successes, there are unprecedented opportunities to do what needs to be done.

If I were invited to speak to young people graduating from high school or college today, I would talk about the successes and failures of my generation, and what those successes and failures mean to their generation. I also would talk about some things that are not unique to any generation, but are universal if too often ignored truths.

When my generation came along, there were certain things we wanted to accomplish. We had come out of the Depression, and we wanted material prosperity. We had fought a terrible war, and we wanted to find ways to prevent more wars. We had begun to glimpse the potential of technology, and we wanted to explore it further. We wanted to find cures for diseases, particularly for the diseases that killed or crippled children. We had experienced the blessings of political and economic freedom, and we wanted to expand those freedoms around the world. We were challenged by our largest racial minority to end political and economic discrimination, to remove racial barriers to the full privileges of citizenship and full access to the American dream.

Today we have unprecedented prosperity, television, computers, jet planes, rocket-powered flights into space, inoculation for polio and diphtheria. Those are some of our successes, and we are proud of them. But if human history teaches us anything, it is that the task of creating a safer, saner, healthier, happier world is never finished.

We are the wealthiest people in the history of the world, but hungry children are a shameful reminder of our failure, of the unfinished business we leave to future generations.

We also failed to consider the consequences of our fantastic technological and economic progress on our natural resources. Thus we have left to subsequent generations, along with the many blessings of technology, a damaged Earth and a polluted environment that must be restored and cleaned up and maintained if it is to continue to sustain life.

We continue to fight wars in pursuit of peace and national security, and we have created treaties and organizations to achieve those goals. But young men and women are still fighting and dying today, and wars and rumors of wars are as prevalent and ominous now as they have ever been. And we probably are less certain of our national security than ever before in our history.

Modern medicine has freed us from disease and pain and early death to an extent undreamed of a hundred years ago. Psychiatry has taught us much about coping with personal anxieties and weaknesses. Yet people continue to risk the blessings of health and sanity and even life itself through drug abuse, including alcohol and unprotected, promiscuous sex. Millions of Americans are without health insurance, and thus without full access to an otherwise magnificent healthcare system.

We have seen the collapse of Soviet communism and the expansion of the frontiers of democracy, but there are new forms of tyranny—including the tyranny of terrorism—that threaten the world.

We have made much progress in eliminating racial discrimination in this nation, but prejudice is still a destructive force and a cruel reality for too many Americans—and not only African Americans.

We have landed men on the moon and a spacecraft on Mars, and the most important consequence of humanity's voyages into space may have little to do with science and technology. It may be that it put the planet Earth in its proper perspective: a relatively minute ball of water and rock moving through the immensity of space. Someone has called it "Spaceship Earth," and that may be the most profound metaphor of our time. We who inhabit this planet are in many ways as interdependent as those who travel together on the Apollo flights. Our oxygen, our water, our food—the ingredients of an environment capable of sustaining life—are limited. They must be conserved and recycled and regenerated.

Our deepening knowledge of the natural environment and its ecosystems also should serve as a metaphor for what I once called our "human ecology"—the networks of human social, cultural and political interaction. Greed, selfishness, hatred, prejudice, intolerance and incivility can corrupt that man-made environment just as toxic wastes can pollute the natural environment. When the rivers and soil and air are polluted, we begin to count the number of fish and birds and trees that die. With the pollution of our social and cultural environment, we see death of such things as integrity, compassion, trust and hope.

As the amazing technological revolutions in communication, transportation and commerce shrink the planet, we are all becoming neighbors. We need to understand that this Spaceship Earth is not likely to be a good place to live for us unless we can make it a good place to live for all those with whom we share it. If we are to find an ultimate answer to the problem of war, short of the end of time, it will have to begin with that understanding.

Politics, For Better or For Worse

The primary mechanism through which we address these concerns is, necessarily, government, and in a representative democracy such as ours, the way government works is determined through politics. Too many people think of politics as something dirty, and they don't want to soil their hands with it. Perhaps politicians have only themselves to blame for that. But there are good politicians, and not so good, just as there are good and bad people in business and the professions. I am proud of the years in which I was a politician. Politics is not—or certainly should not be—just about winning elections. Politics isn't limited to people who run for office. Politics is the network of personal activities through which men and women attempt to cooperatively exercise some control over the forces that affect their lives. In that sense, we are all involved in politics. If we choose to avoid involvement in the affairs of our time, and if we stay home on Election Day, those, too, are political decisions, and we are responsible for the consequences of those decisions.

But if our political system isn't functioning as it should, there is little hope that government will be able to effectively address the concerns of the people, the challenges faced by each successive generation.

As I write at the beginning of a new century, it seems to me our political system is badly damaged and in need of repair. It has been damaged most of all by excessive partisanship. If the primary goal of people serving in the executive and legislative branches of government, at the state or national level, is to assure the success of their party in the next election, and to discredit the other party, more often than not the people lose no matter which party wins.

Too many of our politicians today substitute slogans for intelligent discussion and name-calling for civil, mutually informative debate. Politicians and voters alike seem paralyzed by labels. If an idea or proposal is labeled "conservative" or "liberal," half the politicians and half the voters dismiss it without even bothering to understand it, and the other half embrace it without question. It is all mind-numbing noise and spectacle. In our political lives we function more like rats responding to stimuli in a laboratory than like responsible, mature, thoughtful human beings.

I cannot say exactly who is to blame for that. Perhaps it has to do with the frantic pace of our lives today. Perhaps skilled political advisors have learned how to take advantage of the way television has shrunk our attention span. But blame matters less than responsibility. It is ultimately our responsibility, as citizens and voters, to refuse to play our roles in this farce—to refuse to respond mindlessly to the superficial slogans and the meaningless and sometimes deceptive labels.

It has always been a good idea to be wary of politicians who offer simple answers to complex questions. They do not offer leadership, but demagoguery, and they insult our intelligence. Yet more and more today the only answers we hear are simple enough to fit into a sound bite. We are, or at least could be, the best-informed voters in the history of democracy. Yet, instead of taking advantage of the information available, we take the shortcuts. We declare ourselves Democrat or Republican, liberal, conservative, libertarian, fundamentalist, pro-family, pro-business, whatever. Then we treat politics and government the way we treat a ball game—loyal to our team, to our label, no matter what. But it is not a ball game. It is a process through which a free people supposedly sift through competing ideas and proposals and possible compromises to choose policies that are most likely to work, to achieve our goals—policies that are consistent with our best ideals, our best traditions and our best hopes.

Our best ideals and traditions still matter. For all the amazing changes my generation has seen, certain fundamentals endure, and they are not the exclusive property of any political party, and they are not exclusively liberal or conservative. At our best, we Americans ought to be liberal in dealing with our fellow human beings—slow to condemn, eager to understand, compassionate, willing to respect differences and to judge people as individuals. We ought to be conservative when anyone proposes radical changes in institutions and processes that have provided the best way of life any people in the history of the world have ever known. We ought to be doves in our desire and willingness to work for peace. We ought to be militant in our devotion to a society ordered under law, with equal justice for all.

The law is fundamental. It almost certainly will always include provisions or judicial interpretations with which some of us disagree, but even if we work to change it, we must always respect it. No civilized and free society can exist without the law. Freedom and anarchy are mutually exclusive conditions. Order is essential for freedom. In a room full of people with no law or order, the strongest or biggest person, or the person with a gun, is king. He will make the rules, establish the law, enforce the order. There would be no elections. And that is what happens when law loses its force and order breaks down in a state or nation.

Some political concepts are fundamental. The concept of representative democracy is still the best ever devised for a system of government. The concept of responsible citizenship within a representative democracy is as important today as it ever was. The concept of equality under law is perhaps more important than ever, as relationships between people become more complex in our increasingly complex world.

Certain codes of personal behavior are fundamental. The

American way of life is built on individual thrift, sobriety, hard work, integrity and the Biblical admonition known as the Golden Rule.

The spiritual values that were woven into the founding documents and institutions of this nation have not been made obsolete by our unprecedented material progress. Indeed, the wealth of America has made us the most materialistic society the world has ever known, and that in turn has only exposed the emptiness of lives devoted to unrestrained, instant material gratification.

Trite as it may seem, if there is any truth my generation can pass along to the next generation, and the next, and the next, I would want it to be this: For our lives to have any meaning, we must love each other more than we love material things, and we must love our community and our country more than we love material things. We must value honor and dignity, integrity and justice, more than we value wealth or anything it will buy—including votes.

People with Vision Who Will Not
Accept Defeat

The story is told that out in some sections of the Western United States they drive the cattle into high mountain pastures in early summer. They stay until autumn threatens the high altitudes with cold and snow. Then the cowboys have a roundup and drive the cattle back down to the ranch.

Inevitably, there are some strays, but they are too scattered for a roundup so they send a couple of cowboys into the mountains with a string of donkeys and when they find a steer they tie a donkey to it and turn them loose. At this point the steer acts the way lots of people do when something doesn't suit them . . . when they are forced to associate with a strange animal, especially when it restricts what they consider to be their freedom. The steer takes off across the upland pastures dragging the donkey wherever he wants him to go. But eventually the steer gets tired and stops, and when he does, the donkey, no matter how weary and battered he may be, heads downhill for the ranch and safety. It may be thousands of feet down and miles away, but the donkey knows where the ranch is and however often the steer may take over with its insane violence, the way the world so often does, the donkey always insists on his course of action, and he almost always saves the steer.

None of our problems are insoluble and anyone attempting to do anything is going to be discouraged and disheartened at the apparent lack of progress and success, but we should remember that those people who have accomplished the most knew untold failure and persevered in spite of it.

The immortal Babe Ruth hit 711 home runs in his major league baseball career. It is an all-time record, and perhaps it will never be surpassed. The world remembers these 711 home runs, but it has long since forgotten that along the way he struck out . . . failed 1,504 times . . . also a major league record.

Thomas Edison, the great inventor, was seeking desperately to find the answer to the common light bulb. He tried and tried and yet he failed. One of his assistants said to him, "Mr. Edison, we have tried 1,722 experiments on your light bulb and each has failed. Don't you think we should give up the idea?"

Mr. Edison replied, "Young man, we have found 1,722 ways it won't work. If we keep trying, we shall find the one way it will work."

And one day the world was tremendously enriched when Mr. Edison found the one way it would work.

Observer front page 12-20-71

Taylor A Southern Will Rogers

By HOWARD COVINGTON
Observer Staff Writer

Pat Taylor was pleasant and congenial. He most always is. He likes people and generally the feeling is mutual. A regular Southern gentleman of the old school.

It had been a busy day, politicking in Wadesboro and now ten hours later, Taylor was subdued. He talked quietly with those aboard the single engine Cessna.

Taylor's broken-toned nasal drawl, punctuated with ain'ts, I-do-declares and won'ts instead of weren'ts is natural, just like his wry wit. A friend traveling with him on this day compared him favorably to Will Rogers.

If that be so, then the only differences are that Taylor is Southern grown instead of Oklahoma, more swallow-tail coats and high starched collars than cowboy boots.

Taylor doesn't duck the caricature. In fact he helps promote it with his regular reference that he is "just a country lawyer." And it's not all corn. He has, or at least has had, clients who are strictly downtown but for years the office rent has come from the cases tried in the Anson County Courthouse in downtown Wadesboro.

Today, however, Taylor is less a country lawyer and more a country politician. He is more intent on winning the Democratic nomination for governor next spring than winning a case in court next week.

Sitting in Taylor's law office the muffled clatter of electric typewriters penetrates the paneled walls. They don't intrude on conversation but the telephone, the candidate's crucial link to his supporters, does.

While the Raleigh campaign office of the Taylor campaign is relatively quiet, the Wadesboro branch is going full steam. There are three full-time secretaries responsible for keeping the cards and letters filowing and the schedule in line.

It's been that way since mid-October when Taylor mounted a platform in front of the courthouse and announced his candidacy during the ceremonies at the "Pat Taylor Appreciation Day."

The day was quite an affair complete with free barbecue on the grounds and the high school band. Hometown boosterism at its best. And why not?

Hoyt Patrick Taylor Jr. is a prime beneficiary of Wadesboro and Anson County society. His father was a prominent lawyer, legislator and lieutenant governor under Gov. Kerr Scott.

Taylor's wife comes from a family of Lockharts that have roots as old as the county itself. The youngest of the three Taylor children, for instance, is named for Adam Lockhart, Anson County's voice in the N.C. General Assembly in 1805.

Put it all together and Taylor is a natural. There are some who will probably argue that Taylor's political career was established the day he inherited his daddy's name. Taylor's own casual attitude toward politics and most everything else promotes this conception and to bear him deSee PAT, Page 10A, Col. 1

Today's Chuckle

Wife to husband on Christmas morning: "You angel! Just what I needed to exchange for just what I wanted!"

Lt. Gov. Pat Taylor
...Now Campaigns For Top Job

Observer Photo by Roger Mikeal

N.C. Division of Archives and History

**Lt. Gov. Pat Taylor presiding over the Senate in 1971.
Taylor was House Speaker in 1965–66.**

Who is this kid, and why is he standing on the dais?

even if they were not proactive, you're going to have an agenda to react. They may not have been as tightly defined as some of my ideas, but if they didn't have an idea [of what they wanted to do in terms of policy], they shouldn't have run for office."

Whether they had a clearly stated agenda, other speakers certainly exerted their will through the office. For example, four-term House Speaker Liston Ramsey, a Madison County Democrat, used the power of the office to control the budget process, build the strength of the legislative branch versus the executive branch, and direct numerous multi-million dollar capital projects to western North Carolina. And with Republican Governor James G. Martin in office for two of Ramsey's four terms, the mountain populist had a clear agenda to *oppose* Martin's agenda.

III. Other Institutional Changes in the
Speaker's Office

While the office of the speaker has evolved toward a fully staffed office that enables an independent agenda, there also have been institutional changes that have helped the office consolidate power. Among these are succession (the ability of the speaker to seek more than one consecutive term), the evolution of the speaker's office to a full-time position, and, indirectly, the legislature's removal—or stripping—of certain powers from the lieutenant governor's office.

A. Serving Multiple Terms:
the Most Important Institutional Change?

The freedom to run for the speaker's office more than once often is cited as a way in which the

Christian Science Monitor Amens Pat

An editorial in The Raleigh Times lauding Pat Taylor's statement on law and order in the campaign just needed got an emphatic "Amen" from The Christian Science Monitor, one of the nation's most respected newspapers.

Taylor seeks the Lieutenant Governorship of North Carolina in today's election. Here's the editorial:

Pat Taylor the Democratic nominee for Lieutenant Governor (in N. C.) made a speech recently. What he said should be required reading for every candidate.

Taylor attacked candidates who "use the term 'law and order' as campaign slogans without really explaining what they mean or what they propose to do about it.

"I've never raised this issue of law and order in this campaign because I've never met a person who opposes law and order.

Everyone agrees we should have law and order. But some would have you believe that they will work some kind of miracle and everyone will obey the law or that they would overturn the Supreme Court and the Constitution of the United States and the President and everybody else and leave the enforcement of law and the administration of justice to some kind of supreme police force. But when, in the first place, they couldn't do it, and in the second place, they really would not do it if they could.

"It may be necessary to call some candidate fear preachers easily, but there are those who take the serious issues which confront us and turn them into superficial issues with which they appeal not to your reason, your common sense, but to your anger and reaction.

These are the extremists and some of them are hiding behind a front of moderation and claim the label of conservatives.

"If we are going to talk about law and order, let's be honest about it. How much should be State Highway Pa-

PAT
Starts on page 1

bayonets or chemicals; for even when it is necessary to use them, as it sometimes is, they are at best a temporary solution; and at worst they may degenerate into an emotional outlet for our own frustrations, a cheap substitute for reality and responsibility.

There's only one word to be added to what Taylor said. It is; Amen.

The Nation's Best Urban Policy made Raleigh bigger, better

There's a reason why Raleigh doesn't look like Newark, why Charlotte doesn't look like Detroit, and why no one has ever mistaken Greensboro for Cleveland.

And no, it's not the dogwoods.

It's because North Carolina has been a national pioneer in developing The Nation's Best Urban Policy — annexation.

Annexation doesn't have the sex appeal of such Republican proposals as urban enterprise zones or Democratic ideas such as federal grants to the cities. It merely works. And it's also cheap. Its only drawback is that it takes political guts, which as you may have noticed, is often in short supply.

A strong annexation law is one of the main reasons why North Carolina's cities are among the fastest-growing, have the most vibrant economies, and have the most fiscally sound city governments in

ROB CHRISTENSEN

the country, according to urban expert David Rusk of Washington.

Rusk, the former mayor of Albuquerque, N.M., regularly gives speeches to chambers of commerce and municipal officials in Chicago, Detroit, Philadelphia, Minneapolis and elsewhere. And wherever he goes he tells them "to learn how to organize to do business like the Carolinas."

Since the 1950s, the American dream has been to own a little house in the suburbs with a yard to mow, swings for the kids and a barbecue on which to grill the steaks.

As the middle class migrated to the suburbs, businesses followed. Left behind were the poor folks — often black or Hispanic.

Downtowns in Detroit, Newark, Camden, N.J., and elsewhere are abandoned hulks. There are no sadder sights this side of Calcutta.

But in North Carolina, thanks to The Nation's Best Urban Policy, the cities have grown and absorbed the new subdivisions, shopping centers and suburban office parks into the city limits.

"North Carolina has had the same patterns of growth as the rest of the country — very spread out, low-density growth," Rusk said. "But North Carolina law, more than any other state, encourages your cities to expand with that growth so that Raleigh, Greensboro, Charlotte and the like take into their boundaries much of the new development that occurs."

In most cases, residents about to be annexed pitch a fit. Who wants to pay city taxes, especially when you can take advantage of urban amenities for free? But in North Carolina, cities can annex adjoining areas even if the people living there don't like it.

What would Raleigh look like without North Carolina's strong annexation law? Would the city have been frozen at the Beltline? Would it be surrounded by new incorporated towns called Millbrook, Crabtree or Brentwood?

In his new book, "Cities Without Suburbs," Rusk provides a tale of two cities — Raleigh and Richmond — which are headed in different directions. One city was helped by a strong annexation law, and one wasn't.

The number of people living in the Raleigh and Richmond metro areas grew by the same amount from 1950-90. But because Raleigh was allowed to expand its city limits, Raleigh gained 142,272 people while Richmond lost 27,254 people.

In 1950, Richmond was three times Raleigh's size in square miles. Now Raleigh is significantly larger. (Raleigh grew from 11 to 88 square miles from 1950-90.)

Raleigh is gaining manufacturing jobs, while Richmond's manufacturing base is shrinking. The income of Raleigh residents is growing faster than those who live in Richmond. The income gap between Richmond and its suburbs is growing. There is no such gap in Raleigh.

Richmond is showing signs of a city in decline. The Raleigh-Durham area recently made the cover of Fortune Magazine as the nation's "Best City for Business."

Sometimes far-sighted laws come about in funny ways. The General Assembly passed The Nation's Best Urban Policy in 1959, in part because it wanted the public off its back.

Before 1959, the legislature had to ap-

prove every annexation, which meant hundreds of spitting-mad citizens descending on Raleigh every year. Faced with a problem, the legislature did what it always does — it formed a study commission, which with the help of the Institute of Government in Chapel Hill drafted The Nation's Best Urban Policy.

The key figure in passing the annexation law was state Rep. Pat Taylor of Wadesboro, a 35-year-old lawyer who would rise to become House speaker and lieutenant governor.

Was it controversial?

"Oh my Lord," Taylor, now 70, said last week. "People said this bill was undemocratic. In truth, it couldn't be fairer."

The annexation law, Taylor said, will be one of his lasting legacies.

I don't know this for sure, but I bet Taylor is the only lawyer in Wadesboro (population 3,301) who can claim to be the father of The Nation's Best Urban Policy.

Got a suggestion or just want to talk about Tar Heel politics? Call Rob Christensen at 829-4532.

Pat Taylor A Regular Southern Gentleman Of The Old Sc

Continued From Page 1A

...scribe his own career is to imagine that the first day he entered the N.C. General Assembly was the beginning of a political fall accompli. This is his description:

"I went to the legislature in 1953 and enjoyed it. I thought I was making a contribution to my state and society. I didn't think up the 'idea' of running for the legislature. They came and asked me about running.

"I have not gone out seeking public office."

As Taylor talked, he paced about the office, flicking ashes from his ever-present cigar, pacing from time to time at an interviewer's notes.

"Then I got elected to speaker of the House (1965) and it just goes with that office to run for something else. I dropped out of the 1967 session and I was turning over in my mind whether to run for lieutenant governor. Considering my experience and my age (47) it was natural that people would talk to me about running for governor."

Taylor discounts any adding ambition to hold the office. When he was being courted for the number two there was no doubt supporters were looking at him as a prime candidate for 1972.

"I just don't have any burning ambition to hold the office. I didn't think I couldn't do a first class job but I wouldn't be running for the job."

Press him for an answer and Taylor will admit in spite of his soft sell, it...

Pat Taylor Says:

'It Was Natural That People Would Talk To Me About Running For Governor'

Right now, these people are the key to his efforts and when combined with the notoriety he has received as lieutenant governor the reason that he is considered the leader in a four-way race.

That's why the Taylor campaign has let the organization of the Raleigh office. A regular feature of his gubernatorial politics, is only a skeleton.

One full-time worker is Jim Pate, a former banker from Hendersonville who joined Taylor as an administrative aide last spring. Jerry Shinn, a public relations man, is on part-time loan from radio station WAYS in Charlotte, which continues to pay his salary.

Pat Taylor: 'Down-Home' But Sophisticated

And The Lieutenant Governor Says It's Time To Upgrade His Office

By EDWARD CODY
Associated Press

"Hello!"

He shouted into the receiver the way partially deaf old men used to when wall telephones first arrived down on the farm.

"You, sir. How are you?" The volume dropped. "What can I do for you?"

The answer would determine whether the speaker would be Lt. Gov. H. Pat Taylor Jr. of North Carolina or Pat Taylor.

...smalltown lawyer of Wadesboro.

Taylor plays both roles with the same folksy assurance, salting his speech with downhome "Ah declares" and "ain'ts" but guiding the conversation with a lawbook precision right at home in his sleek office.

But, after two years in the state's second-highest office, Taylor has become convinced the ambivalence is robbing his post of its effectiveness. In an effort to define the job more clearly, he will work for legislation in the 1972 General Assembly to make it fulltime with a substantial salary.

In so doing, he will raise questions that could produce significant changes in the way Tar Heels elect their top executives and in what the executives do during their four years in office.

The lieutenant governor's job has changed in the last decade, Taylor said in an interview, making the officeholder more prominent politically and putting him closer to...

...highest ranking spokesman to make of Taylor virtually a fulltime politician.

"In my office, new letters asking political favors. A young man wants to be a highway patrolman. A corporation head believes state tax laws unfairly penalize his company. A boy wants to be a legislative page, and a girl wants to be a pretty Bowl football game.

Into his office flow letters asking for an appearance when Gov. Bob Scott cannot be there.

"They ask him to go, and he turns them down the next person they ask is the lieutenant governor."

Into his office flow letters asking for a speech: The Rotary Club in Durham needs inspiration—as does the Moore County Democratic rally, the Raleigh urban legislators conference, the New Bern plant dedication.

Turning down the requests would be as simple as dictating an excuse to his state-provided secretary. But representing the state is part of the job. And Taylor concedes he is seriously weighing the race for governor in 1972, when the appearances could become a political savings account.

So the 46-year-old country town lawyer become a man in a hurry, fulfilling a two-page speaking schedule in two months and rolling over the road to Raleigh.

"You add it all up and it's terribly difficult for me to practice law and do this, too," he said.

The practice of law also assumes an added dimension when the lieutenant governor — and maybe the next governor — argues before a state court.

"I can sense it," Taylor said.

"While it really doesn't make any difference, a lot of people — lawyers, litigants and others — think it's strange that the lieutenant governor would be here handling an automobile accident case.

"So why not drop the practice for four years? The answer is as mundane as the grocery bill. The lieutenant governor's salary is $15,000 a year, plus $4,000 a year in expenses and a daily legislative allowance when the assembly is in session.

Raising the salary to the $30,000 range and formalizing the post's fulltime status will be the most immediate goal of the legislation Taylor said he will promote in January.

"I think the governor will join me in this," he said.

The governor's expected support falls in line with Scott's frequent remarks that too much of his time is taken up cutting ribbons, shaking hands and proclaiming special-cause days.

"I have observed the governors of North Carolina," Taylor agreed. "They hardly have time to govern. If the president of a major corporation had to attend the ceremonies and functions a governor does, the corporation would be bankrupt by Christmas."

As a fulltime assistant to the governor, his lieutenant could relieve him of some ceremony and also accept top assignments to guarantee that policy is carried out or to investigate proposed new policy.

"There are many things that need some looking at carefully and closely in order that the governor might formulate policy," Taylor said. "If I were governor today, I could think of a dozen things I would like to put the lieutenant governor to doing."

Lt. Gov. H. Pat Taylor Jr.
... Plays His Two Roles With Assurance

Politician of the past warns that the water's getting hot

Our challenge is to create a political climate in which people like Pat Taylor will want to run, and have a chance to win.

Jerry Shinn

Pat Taylor concluded his remarks to a UNC Charlotte political science class by telling the students how to cook a frog.

If you drop a frog into a pot of boiling water, he said, it will jump out so quickly it won't even be burned. But if you put the frog into a pot of cold water over a low burner, the frog will stay there until it is cooked.

I don't know personally whether that's true or not, since my only experiment involving a frog consisted of dissecting a dead one in a high school biology class. But it doesn't really matter. Taylor, a former N.C. House speaker, former lieutenant governor, semi-retired Wadesboro lawyer and guest speaker one afternoon this week in Dr. Jack Perry's class, was using the frog example to make a point about his subject, "Challenges to Democracy."

Whenever we Americans have faced an immediate threat to our democratic system — Pearl Harbor, for example — we have re-

acted quickly and decisively. Absent a crisis, the danger is that, like a frog in a pot of water heated slowly to boiling, the change is gradual, not even noticing what's happening until it's too late.

It was a good point, and Taylor gave the students a lot of things to think about — serious things, sandwiched between the humorous stories he tells in a deceptively artless, down-home style honed over a lifetime of public speaking and yarn-swapping.

You need to know, before I comment further about Taylor, that during a period when I wasn't a working journalist, I worked on his last campaign, an unsuccessful run for the Democratic nomination for governor in 1972. So I am not altogether objective on the subject. But he was a good, honest, honorable candidate, and I think he would have been a fine governor. I can still imagine him being a fine governor, but I have a hard time imagining him as a candidate in today's political environment, and I suspect he does, too.

He is a lifelong student of his state's history and culture and is steeped in the lore of post-war N.C. politics and government. His father served several terms in the state

Senate and as lieutenant governor in the early 1950s. Pat was elected to the N.C. House in 1954 and served five terms, the last as speaker. Among landmark legislation for which he can claim a fair share of the credit was the state's extraordinary annexation law — a triumph of intellect and sophisticated reasoning in a legislative process where those qualities are all too rare.

Based on his remarks to the class, I don't think Taylor's political views have changed much in the past 25 years. They are still a rather bracing mix of liberal and conservative, principled pragmatism and good-humored tolerance.

Among the things he dislikes in today's politics is the exorbitant cost of campaigning, driven by the cost of the television commercials. He also dislikes polls. He asks, in effect, why take a poll unless you're willing to modify your own views, abandon your own convictions, to bring them in line with popular opinion to the contrary?

So I suppose he is hopelessly old-fashioned. Yet some of his views, now as 25 years ago, are so advanced as to be almost radical.

For example, a bicameral legislature makes no sense to him, either in Washington or in Raleigh. The idea of a separate Senate in the Congress, he said, was a state's rights tactic and an anachronism in the age of one-person, one-vote.

Noting that some people view the Constitution "as a perfect doc-

ument, and particularly when it meets their purposes," Taylor reminded the students that in the beginning it allowed only white males to vote, and the N.C. Constitution was, by today's standards, even more flawed:

"It provided that no person could hold office 'who shall deny the being of God, or the truth of the Protestant religion, or the divine authority of either the Old or New Testament, or shall hold religious principles incompatible with the Freedom and Safety of the State.'

"The word 'Protestant' eliminated Catholics," he pointed out, "and 'Old or New Testament' eliminated Jews and 'incompatible with the Freedom and Safety of the State' eliminated pacifists such as Quakers and Moravians. . . .

"Democracy should be like a river and not a lake," he said. "It will become stagnant if it stands still. Fundamental principles should be reviewed and new principles considered as times change."

But I'm sure he'd agree that not all change is good, and as I listened to him talk I was thinking that the changes in politics since his political career ended have not been, on balance, for the better.

Consider this:

In 1972, the federal court had just ordered the Charlotte-Mecklenburg schools to bus students as necessary to fully desegregate the system. Other urban systems were facing similar requirements. Bus-

ing was a volatile emotional issue in this state, ripe for political exploitation in that election year. But every one of the four candidates for the Democratic nomination for governor declined to pander to white racism and white fears.

When asked about busing, the two leading candidates, Taylor and Hargrove "Skipper" Bowles, both said there was nothing a governor could do about it, and to suggest otherwise would only raise false hopes and strike sparks in an explosive situation.

Instead, they urged North Carolinians to obey the law, whatever it might be, and they promised, if elected, to make sure students found a good school at the end of the bus ride.

And they never dug up any dirt on each other or attacked each other in their advertising. Amazing. Can you imagine an election today in which all the major candidates behaved that decently and responsibly?

Perhaps the greatest challenge to American democracy is to create a political climate in which more people like Pat Taylor will want to run, and have a chance to win.

Meanwhile, today's hot issues are slowly bringing the political pot to a boil, and we all may be cooked before we know it.

Jerry Shinn is an Observer associate editor. Write him at The Observer, P.O. Box 30308, Charlotte, NC 28230.

Pat Taylor during his years as lieutenant governor

We the People
March 1965